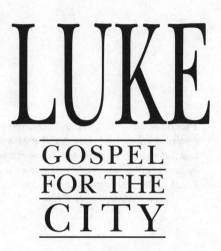

LUKE

GOSPEL
FOR THE
CITY

D0166687

DAVID C. COOK PUBLISHING CO.
ELGIN, IL 60120

This Basic Bible Series study was developed through the combined efforts and resources of a number of David C. Cook's dedicated lesson writers. It was compiled and edited by Larry Sibley, designed by Melanie Lawson and Dawn Lauck, with cover art by Richard Sparks.
—Gary Wilde, Series Editor

Luke: Gospel for the City
© 1988 David C. Cook Publishing Co., 850 North Grove Ave., Elgin, IL 60120. Printed in U.S.A.

Scripture quotations, unless otherwise noted, are taken from the Holy Bible: New International Version, © 1973, 1978, 1984 by the International Bible society, used by permission of Zondervan Bible Publishers.

ISBN: 1-55513-020-8
Library of Congress Catalog Number: 88-70796

Jesus traveled about from one town and village to another, proclaiming the good news of the kingdom of God.

Contents

The One and the Many

How dearly God loves . . . one!
One beloved Son—and He sent Him.
One bleating sheep—and he saved it.
One wayward boy—and He welcomed him.
One missing coin—and He found it.
One beat-up traveler—and he soothed him.
One fallen woman—and He forgave her.
One night in history—and he entered it.
One couple in Nazareth—and He blessed them.
One hour of truth—and He took it.
One cross of death—and he accepted it.
One darkened tomb—and He left it.
One holy will—and He did it.

And yet—especially in the Gospel of Luke—we see Jesus
reaching out to the many, too. He is seen to be constantly
on the move, from town to town; from village to village.
Unfortunately, part of the motivation for that movement
was, as Jesus Himself said: "No prophet is accepted in
his hometown."

How well is he accepted in your hometown?

1
The Nature of Luke's Gospel

Truth to Apply: Luke wants me to know Jesus as the compassionate, Physician-Savior for the urban world in which I live.

Key Verse: It is not the healthy who need a doctor, but the sick. I have not come to call the righteous, but sinners to repentance (Lk. 5:31, 32).

The world is becoming more and more urban. Yet, Christians are often biased against the city. Harvie Conn, a missions professor who spent 12 years as a missionary in Korea (where one of his ministries was to prostitutes) and who lives in a multiracial inner-city neighborhood, points out four factors that make it hard for us to resist our anti-city bias (in *A Clarified Vision*):

1. "Our cultural reading of the Bible" blinds us to its focus on the city. In this lesson we will find that Luke is more interested in cities than we may have realized.

2. "The American dream is a middle-class dream." When the church adopts this dream it blesses materialism, competition and numerical success, and cannot minister effectively to the weak, the defeated, and the nonperson.

3. "Still another roadblock is the privatization of our faith." Rugged American individualism limits our view of discipleship to personal and family life. We lack a kingdom-of-God vision for urban society.

4. "Racism [colors] our vision of the middle-class Dream." The evangelical church move to the suburbs in the last 40 years was really "white flight."

Where do you work? Where do you live? Where do you worship?

Background/Overview: *Luke 1:1-4; 4:38-44; 8:1-4; 5:29-32; 9:18-22*

Luke's writings declare Jesus as the new power in the cities of the world. While Matthew traces Jesus' lineage through the Jewish forefathers, Abraham and David, Luke takes His heritage back to Adam, the father of all humans.

Although the author does not give his name, most scholars think that Luke, a Gentile doctor who traveled with Paul on his missionary trips, is the author of the gospel and its twin, the Book of Acts. Known as "our dear friend Luke, the doctor" (Col. 4:14), He seems to be the one who fits all the clues, found mostly in Acts, where he joins Paul from time to time (Acts 16:10-17; 20:5–21:18; 27:1–28:16). He wrote in Greek, the international language of his day, in a literary style, with rich expression and vocabulary.

Luke's gospel has several main themes. Christ is presented as the Savior of the world; the friend who stands with the poor and powerless, the sick and the brokenhearted. Luke emphasizes the urban setting of Jesus' life and work. Women play a prominent role in this gospel. The Holy Spirit is given an important place. Most important of all is Jesus' purpose to give His life in Jerusalem (9:51; 24:25-27) for the sinners He called to repentance.

Here is an outline of Luke:
Preparation *near* the city, 1:1–4:13
Ministry *in* the cities, 4:14–9:50
Journey *to* the city, 9:51–18:30
Accomplishment *in* the city, 18:31–24:53

Light on the Text

Luke's Purpose and Perspective (1:1-4)

From Luke's opening words we may draw a few conclusions:
1. There were already other accounts of Jesus' life in existence. Also stories about Christ were circulating by word of mouth and letters. Luke had heard his friend Paul preach and seen some of his letters.

2. Luke was interested in writing Christ's story in his own orderly way, perhaps to give his fellow Gentiles a better understanding of what had been recently fulfilled.

3. He had researched his topic well by talking to eyewitnesses, such as Mary, Jesus' mother, and the apostles who were now "servants of the word" (1:2).

Messenger to the City (4:38-44; 8:1-4; 13:22)

In 4:38-44 we have pictures of Jesus' very busy life: a synagogue, a healing, crowds of people, and Jesus seeking solitude. Following such a busy day (4:31-41) Jesus is up at daybreak, praying alone. Perhaps He found a quiet courtyard or empty square in which to pray while the city was still asleep. The people came to try to keep Him from leaving their city. What stands out is His determination to preach in many places, because that is why He was sent.

Luke uses the word for city (*polis*) in 4:43 — "town" in the NIV where Mark 1:38 uses the word "village." Half of the 160 occurrences of *polis* in the New Testament are in Luke and Acts, 39 in Luke alone (Harvie Conn, "Lucan Perspectives and the City" in *Missiology*, XIII, 1). He seems to be deliberately emphasizing the urban setting of Jesus' work and church for his Greek speaking readers who were used to the Greek city-states. In 8:1-4 Luke summarizes how Jesus fulfilled His goal (4:43). Again he uses *polis* pointedly, as he does in 13:22.

When we think of a city in the 20th century, we think in terms of millions of people. But first century Capernaum (4:31) was only about 250 meters by 800 meters with a population of perhaps 1000. This means a population density somewhat like that in a row-house neighborhood of an American city. Houses were close together, not like a suburban neighborhood with detached houses and generous yards. One block of homes in Capernaum, which has been excavated, housed 15 families (130-150 people) in small rooms opening onto a number of internal courtyards (acc. to *New Bible Dictionary, Revised*).

One of the important themes in Luke's gospel is Jesus' love and attention for the poor, the powerless, the disenfranchised people around Him. As Jesus showed His concern for the sick and demon possessed (4:40, 41) He did so in a crowded urban setting. Luke's readers could be assured that Jesus would care for them in their cities.

Our cities, and their suburbs, are filled with the same kinds of people Jesus met: neighborhoods of poor families fighting for survival, government workers who use their positions to cheat or bully citizens, men and women caught in a net of sin—both upper and lower income drug addicts, for instance—and church leaders more interested in building monuments than in being servants.

Christ the Physician (5:29-32)

Capernaum was important enough to have both a customs-post and a military detachment (Lk. 7:1, 2). Levi had been a tax collector. He collaborated with the Roman conquerors and probably overcharged on tax bills, increasing his profit. Because of this he would have been hated by the Jewish leaders (vs. 30). If we were to rank the esteem level for various occupations in the first century, tax collectors would be near the bottom, along with prostitutes and robbers.

Jesus was not sentimental about Levi and others. They were sinners, the ones He came to call to repentance. There is sarcasm in His comment about the "healthy." The Pharisees also were sinners, but they thought they were too healthy to need a doctor. Jesus refused to hold Himself aloof from those who might be considered beneath Him. He welcomed the opportunity to eat with Levi's friends, just as He later went to a Pharisee's home (7:36).

The scribes and Pharisees, with their love of religious nicety and tradition, misunderstood Jesus entirely. For them it seemed He was always breaking rules, meeting with the wrong people—in general, rocking the religious boat.

We might ask ourselves who Jesus' friends would be in today's world. There is an uncomfortable edge to this question. Let's presume that we represent the leadership of the church. We want things to run smoothly. Would we look for wealthy people to build and support the church and professional people to plan and lead the programs? Is it possible that in our drive for a successful church we might lose the humility of Luke's Jesus?

The Christ of God (9:18-22)

This passage is in the center of a group of six paragraphs (9:1-36) that summarize Luke's portrayal of Jesus and His people. We might label the paragraphs this way:

The disciples (His people) preach, 1-6
The king asks who Jesus is, 7-9
The disciples help feed the 5000, 10-17
The disciples answer who Jesus is, 18-22
The disciples are called to suffer, 23-27
The heavenly voice declares who Jesus is, 28-36

The two threads (Jesus and His people) come together in verses 18-22 as Jesus asks the disciples to tell Him, first, who the crowds say He is and then who the disciples say He is. By their confession the disciples identify both their Lord as God's Messiah and themselves as His people called to serve Him by preaching, caring, and suffering.

Shortly after this, Luke tells us (9:51) that "Jesus resolutely set out for Jerusalem," the city where He would fulfill the prophecies of His mother's song (1:46-55). Jerusalem was not only larger than Capernaum (860 meters by 1275 meters, with about 25,000 people, but it was the religious and administrative center of Israel.

As the book moves to its theological climax it also moves to a geographical climax. Luke uses the geographic theme of Jerusalem, with early visits in the first few chapters as a hint of things to come (Simeon's prediction in 2:34, 35 is a good example) and the purpose statement of 9:51 to emphasize the importance of Jesus' death and resurrection.

For Discussion

1. How would you describe Jesus now, after studying Luke's point of view?

2. If Jesus were physically present in your city, where would you find Him eating—and with whom? List some real people you know.

3. What part of your life would be affected most by taking up your cross daily to follow Jesus? What is the hardest thing in your life to "let go"?

Window on the Word

The minister wanted very much to help a young mother

find housing for her and her children. This fatherless family had been house hunting for weeks. They were poor and the mother had no job. The county social service had warned her that if she couldn't supply housing for her family within two weeks, they would place her children in a foster home.

The minister went to his church board. First he persuaded them to complete the purchase of an old house beside the church. For many years the board had considered buying and destroying the house to add to the church parking lot. Then he persuaded them that people were more important than parking. The board voted to refurbish the house and rent it at a low rate to the woman and her children.

The minister then had to appear before a judge to assure him that the woman's housing problem was solved. The judge asked the minister if she was a member of his church. The answer was no. He asked if she attended his church. The answer was no. He asked if she or her children would be attending the Sunday school. The answer was still no.

The judge pushed his chair back and said, "Sir, I've had many ministers come before me over the years to represent people. You are the only one to plead a case for someone when there was nothing to be gained. All the others stood to gain money, favor, or numbers for their churches."

2
The Promise of Jesus' Birth

Truth to Apply: God enjoys working through ordinary people like me to extend His mercy to those who trust Him.

Key Verse: Blessed are you among women, and blessed is the child you will bear!

"Luke is the only one who has recorded for us the outburst of poetry and music in connection with the incarnation. Matthew does not tell us anything about songs; Mark does not tell us anything about songs; John does not tell us anything about songs; but Luke, the Greek, the artist, himself a poet as well as a scientific man when he was investigating and getting these stories, obtained copies of these songs. That is another instance of how the overruling of the Spirit of God allows nothing to be lost. Luke is the instrument, and the right instrument, to give us those early poems and songs. From him we have gained the Beatitude of Elizabeth, the Magnificat of Mary, the Benedictus of Zacharias, and the Nunc Dimittis of Simeon, the Evangel sung by the angel of the Lord over the plains, and the Gloria of the angelic host. Those who love the modes of music will surely linger over these chapters. Luke, the artist, has gathered and collected, under the guidance of the Holy Ghost, the stories which reveal the fact that when Jesus came into the world, poetry expressed itself and music was reborn" (G. Campbell Morgan, *The Gospel According to Luke*).

How does the music in your church help you to worship? What is the worship purpose for each piece of music used in your church services?

Background/Overview: *Luke 1:39-56*

This week's lesson considers the remarkable responses of Elizabeth and Mary to God's plans. In each case God had intervened. Aged Elizabeth's husband, Zacharias, had been performing his duties as a priest in the Temple at Jerusalem when he was confronted by the angel Gabriel (Lk. 1:5-25). He was informed that he and his wife would produce a son, in spite of their age, who would be filled with the Holy Spirit. The Spirit would act as another Elijah to prepare the way for the coming Lord.

As a sign to confirm the angel's promise, Zacharias lost the power of speech until after the child would be born (Lk. 1:20, 22, 64). When Zacharias finished his tour of duty at Jerusalem, he returned to his home in the hill country, and in due time Elizabeth conceived.

Six months after the angel's announcement to Zacharias, the same angel appeared to the betrothed virgin Mary in Nazareth (Lk. 1:26-38). She was a relative of Elizabeth. The announcement to Mary was even more astounding. Although she was not married, she would become the mother of Jesus, the Son of God, through a conception made possible by the Holy Spirit and the power of the Most High.

Light on the Text

Mary Visits Elizabeth (1:39, 40)

Mary lived in the city of Nazareth in Galilee, which was the northern district of Israel. She must have left to visit Elizabeth almost immediately after receiving the angel's announcement, for Elizabeth was already in the sixth month of her pregnancy (1:26). Mary remained with her three months until about the time Elizabeth's child was born (1:56, 57).

Judah is the hilly region in the south, near Jerusalem. Zacharias was one of the hundreds of priests who served in rotation at the Temple. Ancient traditions locate the home of Elizabeth and Zacharias at Ain Karim, about four miles west of Jerusalem. This would have necessitated a journey for Mary of about 90 miles from Nazareth.

The passage does not state the specific reason that Mary went to see Elizabeth, but certain inferences are clear. Mary had been told by the angel that she would be the mother of the Messiah by a virgin birth. To bolster her faith, the angel referred her to the case of Elizabeth, who had already experienced the supernatural action of God in conceiving past the normal age of child bearing. Mary may have regarded the angel's words as a suggestion to visit Elizabeth, so they might confide in each other and rejoice in what God was doing. There was hardly anyone else with whom Mary could share her secret and expect an understanding response. Even her betrothed, Joseph, at first did not understand (Mt. 1:19).

Elizabeth's Blessing (1:41-45)

Even though it is usual for unborn babies to move in the mother's womb by this point in the pregnancy, in this instance the baby's leap is clearly prompted by God, who filled Elizabeth with the Holy Spirit. The arrival of Mary with her greeting brought exultation to Elizabeth that was more than simply human excitement.

With this statement by Elizabeth we have the first recorded prophetic utterance in about 400 years—the first since the last book of the Old Testament had been written. Now, as the fulfillment of the Messianic promise began to unfold, God once again sent His Spirit to empower certain persons to speak His words.

When we compare Luke's account with Matthew's, which follows Joseph's actions (Mt. 1:18-25), it is interesting to note that Luke continues his emphasis on the place women played in God's drama. The first inspired utterance of the New Testament comes through the lips of an ordinary woman and is answered by the praise of another woman (1:46-55).

Elizabeth expressed the great honor she felt at being visited by the mother of "my Lord." This is the same expression that David used of the coming Messiah in Ps. 110:1. Elizabeth recognized that the child Mary was carrying was the Lord, the one promised through the prophets long ago. To say this of Mary's child was to attribute to him a greater position than would belong to Elizabeth's own son. However, she showed no hesitation in accepting God's arrangement.

17

John, her unborn baby, also knew the significance of the moment. His sudden movement in her womb would also confirm her own understanding. Besides praising Mary's child, she also praised Mary's faith, calling her "she who believed." Perhaps she was thinking of the lack of belief shown by her husband, who at this time was dumb because he had questioned the angel's message to him (1:20).

Elizabeth's prophetic word confirmed to Mary that the angel's words would surely come to pass. This assurance would serve to strengthen Mary's trust. Probably she has not yet told Joseph about the angel's visit. If she is at all fearful of his reaction, or that of the general public, this will sustain her during the difficult times ahead. Gabriel had first mentioned Elizabeth to Mary to assist her faith (1:36). Now Elizabeth's words are a further support. God honors and nourishes those who express faith in His Word.

Mary's Magnificat (1:46-56)

Mary's words are called "The Magnificat" from the first word in the Latin translation. Her praise was couched in phrases drawn from the Old Testament and is reminiscent of the prayer of Hannah, the mother of Samuel (I Sam. 2:1-10). Her mind was saturated with Old Testament language. When she spoke her praise, it was largely with words that were already part of the Bible.

When one realizes that Mary had no personal copy of the Old Testament it is clear that she must have listened very carefully to synagogue readings and that Hannah's song had previously made an impression on her. Whether you have a Bible memory program or just remember well what you have studied, Mary's outburst here is a good example of how to learn the Word and use it.

In the Episcopal evening prayer service, this passage is sung by the congregation as a response to the Old Testament reading. Simeon's song (2:29-31), which we will study in the next lesson, is used similarly with the New Testament reading. These songs capture exactly what our response should be to the promise of salvation.

In the opening part of her praises Mary revealed her response to God's dealings. To magnify the Lord is to recognize and proclaim His greatness. Her desire to magnify God is not unlike that of the apostle Paul, who later desired to magnify Christ in his body whether he should live or die (Phil. 1:20).

In the manner of Hebrew poetry, verse 48 is parallel to verses 46 and 47, but expands the thought. It was because God was now sending His Son to act as her Savior that she rejoiced as she did. In view of the excessive honor paid to Mary in some circles, it is noteworthy that she speaks of "God my Savior." She did not regard herself as sinless, but as one needing a Savior.

Mary's thought moved on to celebrate God's greatness and mercy. Her acceptance of God's sovereignty was reflected in the name she used, "the Mighty One." Her reference was not only to sending the long promised Messiah, with all that this implied for peoples and nations (she includes with herself all those who fear or trust God [1:50]), but also to the method which God had chosen. Sending God's Son as a baby conceived by the Holy Spirit without the involvement of a father was an act unprecedented in human history. She resolved this challenge to her faith by viewing this great deed as consistent with a God who is mighty.

Perhaps no three verses in the Bible are as revolutionary as verses 51-53. Each of them is stated in the past tense, even though Mary has not yet given birth. The moment of accomplishment is so near and certain that she senses that history has already turned the corner.

First, God brings about a *moral revolution*: the proud are scattered. While a proper sense of self-respect remains, in a believer sinful pride and independence from God are killed. God resists the proud because they resist Him; He defeats sinful human arrogance.

Second, God brings about a *social revolution*: the mighty on their thrones are put down and those of low degree (like Elizabeth and Mary) are exalted. This is what God did when He defeated Pharaoh and the forces of Egypt on behalf of a slave nation. The powers that human society may amass— think of political, military or social oppression in the world today—are nothing before the living God, who takes pleasure in those of humble and contrite spirit.

Third, the passage speaks of an *economic revolution*: the hungry are fed and the rich are sent away empty. Mary celebrates the time when gross injustice, so prevalent under human rule, will be weighed by God in the scales of His justice. Any economic system must be evaluated by what it does for those least well off.

Mary recognized that what was happening to her and to Elizabeth was God's active intervention in harmony with His promises made long ago to Israel. God's mercy here is not pity, but steadfast love and covenant loyalty. God is always faithful to the covenants in which He has promised certain things to His people.

For Discussion:

1. Suppose you had never before heard of the Christian God. How would this week's Scripture make you want to learn more?

2. How have you seen life begin to be revolutionized when you have submitted to God's working?

3. How would you most like to change over the next few months as an adult Christian?

Window on the Word

The story is told of Muretus, a poor, wandering scholar of the Middle Ages. In Italy he became ill and was sent to a hospital for waifs and strays. While the doctors were discussing his case in Latin (never thinking he would understand them), they suggested that they might use such a worthless wanderer for medical experiments. Whereupon, Muretus looked up and said, "Call no man worthless for whom Christ died."

In contrast, during a plague in Alexandria in the third century, Christians tended the sick and buried the dead while pagans fled like panic stricken animals. Some Christians, who could have escaped the plague, eventually died of the disease themselves. They saw all humans, even those who might never believe and consequently never enter Heaven, as valuable.

3

Acclaim for Jesus' Birth

Truth to Apply: Jesus' birth causes angels, plus men and women like me, to praise God.

Key Verse: The shepherds returned, glorifying and praising God for all the things they had heard and seen, which were just as they had been told (Lk. 2:20).

"The Bible may begin in a garden, but it ends in a city. We've got an urban future whether we like it or not. And what kind of a city is God building? Look at Isaiah 58 which gives us a record. It's going to be a city with a housing policy, an employment policy, and a public health policy, a city where the writer says the children do not die young. That's God's agenda and he's building a city right now. You couldn't honor Him more, I suspect, than to love God and begin to love the city. . . .

"Stop running away from the cities. Move in there with your children. They'll be better off and so will you." (Raymond J. Bakke, "Faithful to the Cities of the World" in *Faithful Witness*, InterVarsity Press).

What can one ordinary family do to serve God in a city? Is it possible to have a godly influence even in one block or neighborhood?

Christ's birth probably took place between 6 and 4 BC, a four-year error having been made by 5th-century Dionysius Exiguus, who transferred dates from the Roman to the Christian calendars. Quirinius was the Roman consul and then imperial legate in Syria between 12 BC and AD 9. Judea was under his administration as part of the Roman province of Syria. The census was a provincial spin-off from a world wide count of Roman citizens and subjects ordered by Caesar Augustus.

Various dates have been observed as Jesus' birthday. December 25 was set in AD 354 by Bishop Liberius of Rome to counteract a pagan festival of Mithras and Saturn. December, however, is Palestine's cold, rainy season, and it is unlikely the shepherds would have been out in the open then. There are sheltered spots where they may have been wintering flocks. December is not impossible, but we have no solid evidence for any date.

Bethlehem, 4.5 miles south of Jerusalem, was the focal point of Messianic hope (Mic. 5:2). The 90 mile trip from Nazareth would have taken about 5 days. The inn was already full. So the weary couple turned to the only space available, a shed for sheltering livestock. The term of Mary's pregnancy and God's time being completed, the birth took place, probably with only Joseph as aide and witness.

Light on the Text

A Surprising Revelation (2:16-20)

Shepherds frequently banded together for company and protection. There were likely several flocks mingled together that night. They were simple, humble outdoor folk who were looked down upon by the rabbis because of their inability to meet ceremonial purification requirements, like constant washing of hands. They had no social standing and were in Bethlehem's "poverty bracket." They were "foolish" in the sense of 1 Corinthians 1:18, open-minded, aware of the nearness of God without tight concepts of how God would act; representatives of those He had come to seek and to save. They were indeed the "poor" to whom Christ came (4:18).

They had just had an unparalleled experience out on the hillside. First they had seen God's glory (2:9), the same glory described by Ezekiel (Ez. 1:27, 28) and seen on the Damascus road (Acts 9:3). Then God's Good News had been proclaimed to them (2:10, 11). The angel announced to them Jesus three roles: Savior, Christ and Lord. *Savior*, a Greek word, implied power to rescue. *Christ*, The Greek form of *Messiah*, pointed to the functions of Prophet, Priest and King, offices initiated by the act of anointing (Lev. 8:30; II Kings 11:12). *Lord* was the equivalent of *YHWH* (*Yahweh*), God's most sacred, unutterable name, symbol of His essence. Christ was, therefore, God Incarnate, as Thomas later acknowledged (Jn. 20:28).

Third, the shepherds had heard the heavenly song (2:14). An army of angelic voices had praised God. Finally, the shepherds had received a commission to seek out the child (2:12). Leaving their flocks they hastened toward Bethlehem (vs. 16). They had no star to follow, as did the Magi (Mt. 2:9, 10). There was no angelic figure to lead the way; they followed only the simple directions the angel had given: the child would be found in a manger.

As promised, the shepherds found the stable. Having worshiped, they left to become Christianity's first evangelists. God used common people to serve Him. Their testimony was not only of what they had seen in the stable: it also proclaimed the angel's message. Micah 5:2 had been fulfilled in their midst.

There were three reactions to the testimony of the shepherds: The townspeople's astonishment (vs. 18), Mary's pondering (vs. 19) and their own joy (vs. 20). The wondering of the people does not imply unbelief, but rather marvel. "Can this be true?" they might have asked. "Has this event really happened—here in our own town?"

Although Mary had known all along who her child was, the reality of it may have become clearer through the shepherd's visit and their story of the hillside chorus. She was putting the details together, like pieces in a puzzle, weighing facts, drawing conclusions, trying to absorb the meaning of the night. We might imagine her remembering the angel's visit nine months ago or Joseph's reactions—and now thinking about how they would rear Jesus together.

The reactions of the shepherds and townspeople may have puzzled her.

The shepherd's joy was without bounds. They had found the angel's news completely true. In sheer delight, they echoed the angel's *gloria in excelsis deo* for all that had happened. They—and the world—would never be the same again.

A Satisfying Fulfillment (2:21-33)

Simeon is quite different from the shepherds, and he meets Jesus under very different circumstances. He appears to have been old, perhaps not far from the usual age for death (vss. 25, 26). He spent his time in the Temple precincts, living righteously and being careful about religious duties.

Mary and Joseph devoutly kept God's Law. They observed the required ceremonies that attended the arrival of every Jewish male child, particularly the firstborn. Jesus was circumcised and named a week after birth. A little over four weeks later He was presented at the Temple when Mary went for ceremonial cleansing.

The first and second rituals took place simultaneously, when Jesus was eight days old (vs. 21). According to Mosaic Law, every boy was circumcised as a symbol of God's covenant with Abraham (Gen. 17:10, 14; Lev. 12:3). This formally marked Jesus as a member of God's covenant people. The ritual was so important that it could even be performed on the Sabbath.

As God, Christ need not have undergone the ceremony. But since He had come "in the likeness of sinful man" (Rom. 8:3) "to fulfill all righteousness" (Mt. 3:15), it was necessary.

At the same time, He was formally named. In Hebrew custom, fathers chose their son's names. Here, however, as with Ishmael (Gen. 16:11), Isaac (Gen. 17:19), and John (Mt. 3:15), there was no choice: He already had been named by God (Lk. 1:31; Mt. 1:21). *Jesus*, the Greek form of *Joshua*, was first used by Moses, who called Oshea, the Ephraimite chosen to spy out the Promised Land, Jehoshua ("savior, deliverer," Num. 13:16).

Greeks reading the Old Testament in their own language would see that the names of the books included Deuteronomy, *Jesus*, Judges. Sometime, try reading a few chapters of the

Book of Joshua substituting "Jesus" in the place of "Joshua", and you will begin to get the effect. If Greek readers of Luke were familiar with the Old Testament character, they would instantly begin to have an idea of what Jesus would do for His people.

The third ceremony, again following Hebrew law (Lev. 12:1-8), was Mary's purification, 40 days after the birth. Though not required to do so, Mary and Joseph traveled the five miles to Jerusalem so that the ritual could take place in the Temple.

The Law required a lamb for a burnt offering to be sacrificed as an act of adoration. A young bird would be the sin offering, bearing the guilt of the worshiper. Poor people, like Mary and Joseph, could substitute a second bird for the lamb (Lev. 12:8), which they did. In a way, though, they *did* bring a lamb—the Lamb of God, who years later would offer Himself at Jerusalem for the sins of the world (Jn. 1:29).

Simultaneous with the mother's purification was the "redemption" of the son. This harkened back to the time of Moses, when firstborn males, who belonged to the Lord (Ex. 13:2, 12; Num. 3:13), could be redeemed or reclaimed by the parents through presentation of an offering (Ex. 13:13; 34:20).

Simeon expected God to fulfil His Messianic promises. Like those of us today who anticipate Christ's second coming, Simeon never lost hope because of God's delay. He looked for Israel's consolation, or comforter (the same root word is used later by Jesus for the Holy Spirit in John 16:7).

Simeon was led by the Spirit, who was upon Him (vs. 25), giving Him special insight (vs. 26), perhaps through a dream, vision or inner conviction. Arriving perhaps at the same time as did Mary and Joseph with the child, the old man took the infant into his arms, a fatherly gesture often performed by rabbis in behalf of God. Here was God, "contracted to a span," in the arms of an old man.

Simeon burst out into a prayer-song, the "Nunc Dimittis" ("now dismiss [your servant in peace]" in Latin). The praise, reminiscent of David's song (Ps. 103), Mary's "Magnificat" (Lk. 1:46-55) and the hymns of the early church (Rom. 11:33-36), poured out the thanksgiving of a joyful, overflowing heart.

The hymn is in three couplets. The first (vs. 29) shows Simeon's satisfaction. Like a watchman having finished his stretch of duty or a slave seeking freedom, Simeon prays for the release of his spirit from the burdens of life.

The second couplet (vss. 30, 31) tells why: Simeon had seen the Messiah with his own eyes.

The third couplet (vs.32) brings together the Jewish nation and the Gentiles. Simeon spoke first of the Gentiles, indicating that the Gospel included them from the beginning. As foreseen by Isaiah (Isa. 42:6; 49:6), Christ came as light to the entire world (Jn. 1:9; 8:12; 12:46).

Mary and Joseph marveled at Simeon's praise. Perhaps, when they heard a stranger recognize the importance of Mary's son, they realized for the first time the scope of His future ministry.

For Discussion

1. As you ponder the common people in this lesson, how is your life similar to theirs? What limitations did they face?

2. What does this passage (Lk. 2:16-33) teach you about giving? About receiving? About praising?

3. What problems does your neighborhood have that frighten or concern you? What do you think Jesus would have you do to serve Him in solving one of these problems?

Window on the Word

An urban, store front church is sometimes one of the best places to see ordinary people serving God. In one east coast city, a former furniture store houses at least five ministries: a thrift shop, a secondhand bookstore, a pre-school through first grade, a housing office, and regular worship services. The building is located near a university, but deliberately on a street frequented by urban poor. Some former students have stayed on to work in this multi-ethnic ministry rather than pursue lucrative careers. Although one might expect an atmosphere of struggle and desperation, what one finds is an abundance of faith and just enough of everything else in God's good time.

4
Jesus Begins His Ministry

Truth to Apply: When I have God's Word in my heart, I am able to resist temptation.

Key Verse: Jesus returned in the power of the Spirit, and news about Him spread through the whole countryside (Lk. 4:14).

". . . People outside find it difficult to imagine what prison life is like. The situation in itself—that is each single moment—is perhaps not so very different here from anywhere else; I read, meditate, write, pace up and down my cell—without rubbing myself sore against the walls like a polar bear. The great thing is to stick to what one still has and can do—there is still plenty left—and not to be dominated by the thought of what one cannot do, and by feelings of resentment and discontent. I'm sure I never realized as clearly as I do here what the Bible and Luther meant by temptation. Quite suddenly, and for no apparent physical or psychological reason, the peace and composure that were supporting one are jarred, and the heart becomes, in Jeremiah's expressive phrase, 'deceitful above all things, and desperately corrupt; who can understand it?' It feels like an invasion from outside, as if by evil powers trying to rob one of what is most vital" (Dietrich Bonhoeffer, to his parents in May, 1943, from *Letters and Papers from Prison*).

What do you do when temptation comes?

Jesus' public ministry begins in the middle of Luke 4, so everthing up to that point is preparatory. Luke uses the first three chapters deliberately to intertwine the stories of Jesus and John the Baptist, especially the accounts of their births. In Luke 3, as John's ministry reached a high point, the Holy Spirit descended upon Jesus, signifying the start of His public ministry after 30 years of private life and silence.

Led by the Spirit, Jesus goes into a different part of the wilderness to contemplate His coming ministry. He fasts, as Old Testament prophets often did, and is, in this crucial time, also tempted by the Devil.

Our passage divides into three parts, one for each temptation. The Devil makes a statement and Christ responds with a quotation from Deuteronomy. The Devil, in his subtle attacks, implies more than he states. Christ penetrates through the sugarcoating and deceit to the heart of what Satan is proposing.

These temptations develop a number of themes. They offer what appears at first glance to be an easy way out of a problem (hunger, need for authority, authentication of ministry). They explore sources of power (Christ, Satan, the Father). They pose a misuse of something (Christ's power, His ministry, God's care). They attack the Son's identity and the Father's integrity.

Light on the Text

A Table Before Me (4:1-4)

Novelist Chaim Potok has pointed out that all beginnings are hard. Beginnings are often crucial, too. Jesus was launching His public ministry. A mistake would have been disastrous, and Satan attacked with force. At the end of the temptations, having failed this time, "he left him until an opportune time" (v. 13).

Luke had earlier highlighted Jesus' identity as the Son of God at His baptism, which was the culmination of John's ministry of preparing the way (3:22) and at the end of Jesus' genealogy (3:37). The Devil's first words are, "If you are the Son of God . . ." as if to say, "Let's prove it." Jesus' answers to each challenge show that He is indeed the Son of God.

Verse 1 of our passage corrects a myth. We may think troubled days means we are out of touch with God. Here Jesus, full of the Holy Spirit, is assailed by Satan. We must not think that opposition means we are "out of the will of God." In a world where Satan is so active, it may be our godly *obedience* that leads to trouble! Note that Jesus was led in the desert by the Spirit.

Christ rejected the suggestion to turn a stone to bread. It might not appear wrong to satisfy a legitimate human need, such as hunger, by divine power, but Christ's answer gives us the clue to the error. He referred to Deuteronomy 8:3. God had taken Israel into the wilderness to show them He could be trusted to provide His own people with food, protection, and guidance. But when they were hungry, He did not give them bread. Rather, He provided a different food, manna. The kind of food and the means of giving it were not crucial; the point was that God is good and provides for His people.

For Jesus to turn a stone to bread would be to say, "I doubt the Father's care, so I will trust myself and care for my own needs." Yet He rejected this tactic. He was the Son living in obedience to the Father. The passage He quoted from Deuteronomy, "Man does not live on bread alone," goes on to say, "but on every word that comes from the mouth of the LORD."

Christ often related His ministry to the written Word. Scripture was to His ministry what the articles on incorporation are to a company. They provided Him with an indisputable basis of authority for refuting the Devil. Further, as the representative human being, Christ submitted to procedures that we in our frailty can duplicate; He reached outside immediate circumstances to the broad, eternal perspective of the Bible.

A God Above Me (4:5-8)

For Christ to submit to Satan would have meant for Him to change the nature of His ministry from saving to enslaving us. Without the cross, His ministry would have been lost and, under Satan's thumb, illegitimate. But Christ "learned obedience from what he suffered" (Heb. 5:8). In fact, the temptation account in Luke bears striking similarity to the opening chapters of Hebrews, especially Hebrews 2 with its emphasis on angels, temptations, and suffering. "Because he himself suffered when he was tempted, he is able to help those who are being tempted" (Heb. 2:18).

Paul says in Romans 5:3 that suffering leads to the development of character. In fact, it was on this very issue of whether the Messiah must suffer that Christ and Peter disagreed after the great confession of Matthew 16. Peter could not imagine a Messiah subjected to death on a cross. Later, Peter also was able to teach about the place of suffering in the life of Christians, as 1 Peter 3:12-19 shows.

Christ, in answering the Devil, went again to the heart of the matter. It is an affront to God to worship anyone else, and He used Scripture to support this. He brushed aside Satan's limited power, not even disputing it. Worship and service are the same allegiance, so in order to declare God's worth, according to the Bible, we serve Him obediently. Disobedience, then, is ultimately a rejection of God's worth. Worship is not something we mainly "do in church" but is a lifestyle of submission based on God's worth.

The word *illusion* describes much that is wily about Satan. He wants us to believe an illusion of some sort. To Eve he posed the illusion that she would become like God if she ate from the forbidden tree. He led King Saul to think he would succeed even though he ignored God's words transmitted through Samuel. Here in Luke 4 he offers an illusory power and glory. No doubt Satan could free Jesus from hardships: the physical labor that goes with itinerant preaching, the emotional drain of involvement with people and their suffering, the persistent opposition of Jewish leaders, and the fickleness of the people. Satan could give a kind of acclaim, but not one suitable to exchange for the glory to come to Christ by way of the cross, or due Him as God the Son.

A Faith Within Me (4:9-15)

Satan now brings Jesus to Jerusalem, the city where Jesus had been presented to the LORD (2:22) and where He had listened to the teachers, asked them questions and amazed them with His understanding (2:46, 47). Luke arranges the temptations in a different order from Matthew, who places this one second. Jerusalem is where the final drama of redemption will be enacted and where the disciples will return in the last verses of the gospel to praise God. The sequence of the temptations anticipates the final outcome. Because Jesus faced this one successfully, He would return to the Father after His death and His followers would continue to serve God.

We have seen a pattern emerging. Jesus, the Son of God, answered Satan not with His own wise words, but with those of Scripture. Do we find guidance from this in facing our own crises? We believe in the authority of Scripture partly because of the example and teaching of Christ, our Teacher and Lord. We should go the next step and use it as He did.

There are common sense rules that separate the use of Scripture from its misuse. Today we are flooded with sects that fasten on one verse or another as proof for this or that teaching in conflict with the general thrust of Scripture. The arrogance of Satan shows how he supported twisted interpretations. Here in the sight of God, author of Scripture, and of Christ, Satan misused a promise meant to calm our fears when trouble comes upon us. It would be improper to manufacture a crisis to see if God will really come through, as Satan suggested here. Presumably the temptation was for Jesus to take another easy way out—a quick dramatic act before the Jerusalem crowds to establish His Messianic credentials.

Satan tried to use Scripture to undercut Christ's relation to the Father and lure Him into a cheap act that would either show doubt in God's power, or misuse of it. In Psalm 91, which Satan quotes, we are in a Creator/servant relationship. God is not to be maneuvered into defending Himself, or His power, nor His care for us. We are His servants. In His connection with Christ as the perfect human and the representative servant, God's integrity is not to be questioned.

From Christ's answer, it is clear that if He were to leap from the Temple He would be testing God (v. 12). As we walk in God's will, He supports us. We do not contrive situations where God is put on the spot. When we are challenged in carrying out His orders, we trust Him to protect us.

In verses 13-15 we learn that the temptations came to a temporary end. Jesus, still empowered by the Spirit, went north into Galilee and ministered effectively in the beginning of His public activities. It is interesting to note that in the next incident (4:16-30) Jesus is rejected by His own townspeople. The temptations and His handling of them prepared Him for this disappointment. He had clearly settled whom He trusted and how He would proceed.

For Discussion

1. Share an experience of being tempted, but overcoming that temptation. What was the place of Scripture in your experience? What did you learn about yourself?

2. How would you counsel someone who is plagued by a "besetting sin" (i.e., he or she keeps on going back to that sin even after repentance and determination to change)?

3. In what ways do you sense that God is helping you overcome temptation? What advice do you have for others?

Window on the Word

Miltons *Paradise Lost* tells the story of the fall of Adam and Eve. When he came to tell of regaining Paradise, (in *Paradise Regained*), Milton based that poem on Luke's account of Jesus' temptation, seeing Jesus as the second Adam, along the lines of Romans 5:15: ". . . how much more did God's grace and the gift that came by the grace of the one man, Jesus Christ, overflow to the many!"

One section of the poem provides a comment after the Devil left Jesus, showing the implications of Jesus' refusal of the temptation:
". . . now thou hast aveng'd
   Supplanted Adam, and by vanquishing
Temptation, hast regain'd lost Paradise,
   And frustrated the conquest fraudulent."

5

Teaching About Forgiveness

Truth to Apply: When I realize how much I have been forgiven, I am able to love and forgive others.

Key Verse: Therefore, I tell you, her many sins have been forgiven—for she loved much. But he who has been forgiven little loves little (Lk. 7:47).

Modern suburbia provides a setting for a painful reality. Many suburbanites feel they "have it made" because they have a house, family, some grass and trees, and yet they may sense that there "ought" to be more satisfaction and fulfillment in daily living.

Something has gone wrong. What is it? One answer is that, by flocking to an area where people are much alike, a person can lose the vitality that comes from interacting with those who differ from him or her. A typical town tends to be of the same race, social class, education. People dress the same. Just look at the commuter crowd getting on the train—alike right down to their briefcases and Reeboks!

Our tendency to prefer people like ourselves makes us distrustful of those who are different. Because they deviate from our norms we think of them as "deviants." A "we vs. they" mindset is established.

It wasn't just Simon the Pharisee who erected barriers and froze others in a never-to-thaw block of ice. Simon's self-righteousness shows how blind he was to his own behavior. We do this, too, and then wonder why people may resent us.

Where are you most likely to meet people whose culture or lifestyle are different from yours? What happens in these encounters?

Background/Overview: *Luke 7:36-50*

In Luke 7 the author describes the faith of the centurion (7:9); the response of the people to the raising of the widow of Nain's son ("A great prophet has appeared among us," 7:16); the question and the testimony of John the Baptist (7:18-28) along with the fickle nature of the crowds (7:31-35); and this story which contrasts the gratitude of a woman with rejection by the Pharisees. These events prepare us for Peter's confession that Jesus is the Christ in chapter 9. The contrast of faith versus rejection becomes even clearer in chapter 8 with Jesus' parable of the soils (vss. 4-15).

The Pharisees rejected God's counsel when they heard Jesus' words, but the people and the publicans (tax collectors and others regarded as notorious sinners by the Pharisees) acknowledged that God's way was right. John the Baptist had prepared the way, and now the Lord came with grace. People like the woman of Luke 7:36-50 responded with gratitude and joy.

Light on the Text

An Outpouring of Love (7:36-39)

Luke's sharp words about the Pharisees (they "rejected God's purpose for themselves," 7:30) begin to get personal in verses 36-39. No less than four times he notes that Simon is a Pharisee.

The woman would have found it easy to get close enough to Christ's feet to wash and anoint them. Remember that in Eastern culture, dinner guests left their sandals at the door and reclined around a low table, lying on their sides. The bare feet of each guest were readily accessible to anyone standing behind.

In all fairness to Simon, it is easy to understand his alarm as he smelled the fragrance of the perfume and turned to see what was happening. An immoral woman was stroking Jesus' feet—even kissing them. "What's going on here?" he must have thought, reacting out of his extreme concern with propriety.

At any rate, Simon did a slow boil. The original language of verse 39 makes it clear that the clause "if this man were a prophet" is not just a simple conditional statement. It might better be understood, "If he were a prophet, and I conclude from these circumstances that he is not, . . ." Prophets were supposed to be indignant over sin. Didn't he have the insight to spot the unrighteous? Prophets were supposed to be like Simon—respectable.

The woman appears to have been a prostitute ("had lived a sinful life"). In those days strangers could come into a home during a feast to talk to guests, but for a prostitute to publicly enter a Pharisee's house would be considered improper. She probably had planned only to anoint the feet of Jesus, but was so overcome by His mercy and by the guilt of her past that she broke down and cried.

Her tears fell on His feet, washing them as a thunderstorm washes the earth (the word is used this way elsewhere). In her embarrassment, she lets down her hair (by custom considered an immodest act) to dry His feet so she could apply the perfume. Overcome again, she repeatedly kissed His feet much as the prodigal's father repeatedly kissed his son (Lk. 15:20).

Simon sees the anointing and is revolted by it. "This man" (vs. 39) suggests contempt; "what kind of woman she is" suggests the same. He divided his contempt between the woman and Jesus—a bad prophet and a bad woman. As with the Pharisee in the parable involving a publican, Simon was grateful he was not like them. However, Simon was an open book to Jesus.

A Story With a Stinger (7:40-43)

"Simon, I have a story . . . ." Stories are often better than lectures. Jesus could be direct ("Woe to you, Pharisees" in Mt. 23), but He had many arrows in His quiver and used them all. One is reminded of the Old Testament, when David arranged Uriah's death so he could take Bathsheba. Nathan told David a story about a rich man with many sheep who took away from a poor man his only ewe lamb. Here in Luke Jesus tells a story to make His point.

Two men owed sums to a moneylender (vs. 41). One debt was ten times greater than the other. The actual dollar amounts in today's economy figure out to approximately $32,000 and $3,200—at $8.00 per hour for eight-hour days. (A typical Palestinian farm hand could earn one *denarius* per day.) The moneylender "graced" them both.

"Canceled" (vss. 42, 43) is the verb form of the noun translated "grace" in the New Testament.

"I suppose" introduces Simon's reluctant answer. Maybe he saw where the argument was headed and wanted to avoid getting caught. Or, he may have been slow in reacting to Jesus' initiative after he, Simon, had written Him off as a phony prophet. Possibly, he was just so arrogant that he hardly deigned to answer at all.

A Case Dismissed (7:44-50)

Note Luke's dramatic sense. Only now does he tell us the details of Jesus' reception (or lack of reception!) when He arrived at Simon's house. By surprising us in verses 44-46 and letting Jesus do the describing, He drives home the point with greater emotion and yet with economy of language.

It was customary in those days, when people walked unpaved roads in open sandals, for a host to set out water for washing off the dust (or to order a servant to do the washing). Simon had not. And a host treated an honored guest with a kiss. Simon had not.

Point by point, the woman had fulfilled the spirit of gracious hospitality. Simon must have been shattered. Control of the situation had passed from him to Jesus and he scarcely knew how it had happened. Water, kiss, and oil were the key words in Jesus charge. "You did not give me . . . but this woman . . ." spoke volumes.

The woman's gratefulness led to godliness; the man's thanklessness led to godlessness. Touched by a sense that Christ had truly forgiven her, this woman poured out the balm of salvation—devotion to Christ.

Verse 47 ties it all down. Jesus says, in effect, "When it comes to sins, Simon, I don't deny her wickedness. But notice one thing: they are forgiven." Note that Christ does not continue the parallel in verse 47 to say that Simon's minor sins are forgiven, too.

Jesus, in conclusion, sets out to reaffirm to the woman, who is hardly able to grasp the fact of her forgiveness, that she is now a friend of God.

What is the place of faith and peace in all this? Jesus answers in verse 50. Faith was the woman's confidence in Jesus that led her to seek Him out. It also marked the state of repentance. Faith and repentance are two sides of one coin and never exist separately in true conversion. The acceptance of Christ led to forgiveness, and realization of that forgiveness led to love.

For Discussion

1. Why do we so often put people into pigeonholes and assume they can never change?

2. What clues from this passage might help you be more loving toward someone you consider to be "from the other side of the tracks?"

3. How can you become more loving towards people with whom you don't tend to be naturally drawn toward?

Window on the Word

In the inner-city of Philadelphia, housed in the former home of a gangster, the Center for Urban Theological Studies (CUTS) trains leaders for the urban church. It also embodies a unique partnership between black and white Christians, urban and suburban churches. Reconciliation is a major agenda at CUTS, equal in importance to the task of education.

Early in the formative stages the bi-racial Board made a frank assessment and affirmed that the responsibility for the divisions which exist between the black and white churches lays at the feet of the white church. The preamble to the CUTS constitution asserts that, since the days of antebellum slavery, the white church has built walls of alienation that have separated her from the poor and minority church community. This pattern lasted for two centuries, hindering ministry in the city, denying the unity of the Body of Christ and creating an illusion within the white church that white congregations are self sufficient and do not need their black brothers and sisters.

The genius of CUTS is a partnership reflected in Board structure where half the members come from the city and half from the suburbs, and in the administration where positions of authority are held by blacks as well as whites. Partnership is also exhibited in joint ownership of the

Center and its programs by the same cross-cultural mix of churches; each group of churches contributes its strengths.

The center works hard to overcome years of abuse received by minorities from the educational system. Consequently, basic curriculum decisions are made jointly by urban and suburban representatives and individual programs are tailored to individual student needs. Reconciliation occurs in the classroom as students from different races and church traditions learn together under a multi-cultural faculty and in an environment where God's image in each person is respected.

6

Teaching About Compassion

Truth to Apply: My neighbor in need is a friend indeed.

Key Verse: He answered: "Love the Lord your God with all your heart and with all your soul and with all your strength and with all your mind"; and, "Love your neighbor as yourself" (Lk. 10:27)

Some years ago a professional athlete was explaining why he had rejected Christianity. "The Bible had no further meaning for me," he said. "The Bible and its teaching had produced all these hate-filled people . . . . It seemed to me that there was nothing in the world as unlike Christ as Christians." How tragic. Because of the racial hostilities he had experienced as a young man, he was blaming the church. And yet, he did have a point. Many Christians had come across to him as hypocritical and smug. One church in a certain city painted its buses, "The Friendliest Church in Town," yet it was no secret that its members were friendliest toward those of the same race.

"Red and yellow, black and white — all are precious in His sight" goes the song. It is still a challenge for many of us to feel the same way.

By the reference to a Samaritan in an audience of Jews, Jesus made clear that those of races other than our own are nevertheless our neighbors. Two thousand years later, the concept is still hotly disputed. Neighborliness is easy in theory, but difficult in practice. Who is your neighbor, and why?

39

The roots of the Samaritans are something of a mystery, for the ancient records we possess come mostly from their enemies. James Kelso states, "The Samaritans are usually assumed to be the descendants of intermarriage between the Israelites of the Northern Kingdom and foreign colonists brought into the land by the conquering Assyrians in 721 B.C." (*An Archaeologist Looks at the Gospels*). The first century province of Samaria lay between Galilee in the north and Judea in the south.

The Samaritans' Bible consisted of their own version of the first five books of the Old Testament. The Samaritan temple, perched atop Mount Gerizim (Jn. 4:20, 21), was their counterpart to the Jewish Temple in Jerusalem and was destroyed by the Jewish John Hyrcanus in 128 B.C.

Around 180 B.C. another Jesus, called the Son of Sirach, spoke of "the foolish nation which dwells in Shechem"—the Samaritans. By contrast, the Lord Jesus Christ mixed freely with Samaritans. He talked privately with a woman of Samaria by Jacob's well and even did a most un-Jewish thing, spending two nights in a Samaritan village (Jn. 4:7-26, 40).

Luke placed the Parable of the Good Samaritan in chapter 10, where it contrasts with the rejection recorded in chapter 9. Throughout this section Luke is contrasting Jesus and the Jews, and Samaritans and Jews, like a painting that repeats the contrast between light and dark until it seems to vibrate with conflict.

Light on the Text

The Ping-Pong Match (10:25-29)

In ancient Jewish society, civil law and religious law came from the same source, namely, the five books of Moses. Jews felt the need for professional specialists to interpret their Law, which regulated their whole life. The "experts in the law," or "teachers of the law" (5:17), were really theologians or Biblical scholars.

While the scholar's motives were suspect, his question ("Teacher, what must I do to inherit eternal life?") was excellent.

Jesus' question turned the tables; the questioner became the answerer. The Law expert's answer was impeccable (which shows that you can be right when you are wrong!). He stitched together Deuteronomy 6:5 and Leviticus 19:18 for his answer. In fact, E.M. Blaiklock noted that "it is ironical that Lev. 19:18 . . . was probably worn in a tiny leather case on the scribe's waist when he posed his question" (*Commentary on the New Testament*).

Jesus told the theologian he had answered "correctly" (Greek *orthos*, from which we get *ortho* dontist, a tooth corrector; *ortho* dox, correct doctrine, etc.). The expert had asked what he should "do" (vs. 25, the Greek tense implying some single, crisis action), whereas Jesus said, "Do [the Greek tense indicating a continuing life process] this and you will live" (vs. 28).

Obviously, the trickster theologian's trap had failed to catch his quarry. Therefore, he tried to "justify himself" (vs. 29; contrast Lk. 18:14) by hunting for a legal loophole. It was as if he had asked in verse 29, "Well, to whom do I have to be neighborly?" (which really meant, "To whom do I *not* have to be a neighbor?"). He was reaching into the age-old bag of tricks: if all else fails, start an ethical argument or split philosophical hairs. But his trick backfired. Jesus told a story to interrupt the ping-pong match of wits.

The Unparalleled Parable (10:30-35)

Jerusalem is about 2,600 feet above sea level. Thus the road "down from Jerusalem to Jericho" (vs. 30) "descends some 3,300 feet in the course of 17 miles" (I. Howard Marshall, *Commentary on Luke*). The road was even called "the bloody way," because the many caves nearby made it a roost for robbers, even into modern times.

"Robbers" (vs. 30) may seem a bit tame, suggesting pickpockets or through-the-window burglars. But these attackers were bandits lurking along the highway who beat up their victim, made off with his money and left him "half dead."

Jericho "was the residence of about half of the priestly orders," states Earle Ellis (*The Gospel of Luke*). No wonder, then that a Temple priest was the victim's first passerby.

41

Note that he, too, was "going down." He was probably coming home from Jerusalem to his off-duty residence and thus not in a hurry to get to work at the Temple.

I.H. Marshall states that there were "some 18,000" priests. Consequently, to serve as Zacharias did (in Lk. 1) was for many priests a once-in-a-lifetime opportunity. Who knows? Maybe this priest was homeward bound from his lifetime highlight.

What thoughts may have gone through the priests head? Maybe he thought, "I don't want to defile myself by touching this dying man; he's obviously past helping" or, "He must be a decoy; if I stop, they'll jump me, too."

Levites are mentioned elsewhere in the New Testament only at also coming from the priestly tribe of Levi. Both priest and co-worker "passed by on the other side" (vss. 31, 32). These first two travelers had been selected by Jesus as He crafted the story because they would be held in high popular esteem and would be most expected to love God and neighbor.

When the third traveler made his appearance "the hearers would assume that the villain of the piece had arrived upon the scene" (William Barclay, *And Jesus Said*). After all, there was no such thing as a good Samaritan (remember the American settlers comments about good Indians!). But one can easily imagine eyes and faces registering shock when Jesus made the Samaritan the *hero*. He deliberately created a startling effect.

The Samaritan could have muttered to himself, "The guy on the ground is obviously a Jew. After what they've done to us, I wouldn't touch him with a ten-foot pole. Even if I did help he'd probably spit in my face." But instead, he tried to undo what the bandits had done. He put himself totally at the disposal of the helpless one.

In verses 34, 35 Luke uses several Greek words found only here in the New Testament: "bandaged," "wounds," "pouring on," "inn" (different from the "inn" of 2:7), "took care" (only in this passage and I Tim. 3:5), "innkeeper" and "extra expense." These unique words seem to imply that what this individual did was unprecedented.

Along with bandages, the Samaritan supplied "oil and wine" (vs. 34). For surface ulcers the ancient physician Hippocrates had prescribed, "Bind with soft wool and sprinkle with wine and oil" (A.T. Robertson, *Word Pictures* in the New Testament, II). Thus, Hendricksen writes, he administered "first aid by washing his wounds with wine (because of its alcoholic content being a disinfectant and antiseptic), and by pouring into them soothing oil, acting as a kind of salve" (*The Gospel of Luke*).

To the provision of bandages and beast the Samaritan added room and board. The "silver coins" are the Greek *denarius*, the going pay for laborers per day. To this basic outlay of unbudgeted funds the Samaritan promised to cover any extra expenses the innkeeper might incur (vs. 35).

The Punch Line (10:36, 37)

Once more Jesus issued a question (vs. 36). The theologian was caught. Obviously the lawyer couldn't answer, "the pious John 1:19 and Acts 4:36. They were Temple helpers and custodians as well as right-hand men to the priests, priest" or "the faithful Levite." He had to admit the neighbor was the one who took action, even if he was a Samaritan.

As Bible scholar Alexander Maclaren worded it, "It is better to ask, Whose neighbor am I? than Who is my neighbor?" The expert in the Law really wanted to pick and choose whom not to love. He wanted to live in the land called Theory, while the Lord directed him to the land called Real Neighborliness.

The lawyer managed to give the right answer without using the word Samaritan. Even though his attitude was wrong, he pointed to mercy, sometimes at risk, as the essence of neighborliness. In telling this story Jesus made a double point: The Kingdom of God is full of surprises (the "wrong" people do the right things) and Kingdom ethics are often a reversal of the usual way of doing things (mercy, sometimes, instead of piety).

For Discussion

1. How did Jesus refocus the lawyer's understanding of "neighbor," and how has this changed your understanding of your neighborhood?

2. Who are the Samaritans in today's world? In what ways are Kingdom people reaching out to them? Do you have

ideas about how your own church could get more involved in such outreach?

3. Why do we so often wall ourselves off from getting involved with people who need help? Share your own experience.

Window on the Word

In Mendenhall, Mississippi, a building called Samaritan Inn is part of the community complex known as the Voice of Calvary (VOC). Other buildings on the grounds related to the ministry of VOC include a farm, health clinic, cooperative store, Bible institute, remodeled houses and gymnasium. Workers include an X-ray technician, medical doctor, reading tutors, and others. The challenge of all this is to bring a degree of Christian compassion to a community of needy people.

The ministry is the result of the dream of John Perkins, a black man whose faith in Jesus Christ has not been a bed of roses. He has been both victim and good Samaritan over the years. After watching his brother die from a police shooting, he left Mississippi for the West Coast. He later become a Christian, and in 1960 he decided to return to rural Mississippi, even though it would be dangerous, to begin a ministry of community transformation.

During the course of his ministry, Perkins has healed a lot of wounds. He once taught Bible stories to more than 10,000 school children a month. Underprivileged students have been helped financially to go to college, about half of them to Christian colleges. In dozens of ways John Perkins has translated his born-again faith into rejuvenating Christian leadership in his community. Luke 10 has been revisited.

7
Teaching About Priorities

Truth to Apply: When I am prepared for Jesus to return suddenly, I will curb my desire to accumulate wealth.

Key Verse: You also must be ready, because the Son of Man will come at an hour when you do not expect him (Lk. 12:40).

"To be human is to be hungry. All children are hungry. They are born hungry. Most children are always hungry. Some children are starving. It is terrifying to see a starving child. It is more terrifying to be a starving child. Starvation is horrible. To be without food is a hell.

"To have experienced the Christ, to have encountered Jesus of Nazareth, to have run headlong into the person of God in the flesh must have been like stepping into the path of a hurricane. No one would do it intentionally. Human beings do not seek out hurricanes. Hurricanes happen. Suddenly. Often without much warning. If we can avoid 'being there', we do. If we can't, we don't. It is really almost as simple as that. To experience the Christ is to run headlong into the path of a hurricane. Jesus said: 'Man cannot live by bread alone' " (Martin Bell, in *The Way of the Wolf*).

In what ways are you trying to live by bread alone? Are we trying to solve the problems of the world by bread alone?

As Jesus proceeded with His ministry, teaching the crowds and showing the true nature of God, He worked in greater depth with the inner circle of disciples. His teaching continued to stir up the Pharisees and scribes who were trying to trap Him into saying something incriminating (Lk. 11:54).

In this discourse, we find Jesus speaking to a crowd so great that the people were stepping on one another. He warns the disciples concerning hypocrisy (12:1-3), admonishes them about the opposition they must face (12:4-12), quiets their anxiety about basic material needs and asks them to give away their property (12:22-34). Then He urges them to be faithful in light of the coming of the Son of Man (12:35-48) and warns them of the coming crisis, which will involve division in families (12:49-53). Jesus introduces the teaching about material needs and property by a warning to the crowd about the desire to accumulate property (12:13-21). He continues the eschatological ("end times") warnings to the disciples with an eschatological warning to the crowd (12:54-13:9). Thus, the words addressed to the crowd are related in topic to the more predominant instructions to the disciples (see Robert C. Tannehill, *The Narrative Unity of Luke-Acts, Volume 1*, p. 242).

In the middle of these crucial teachings, Jesus was interrupted by a personal question from someone in the crowd. The question seemed unrelated to what Jesus had been saying. In fact, it is easy to suppose that the person merely wanted to get a problem solved.

Instead of directly answering the question, which was inappropriate for a public teaching session anyway, Jesus took the opportunity to go beyond the question to the real problem and to teach the crowd further principles of the godly life.

Light on the Text

The Collector (12:13-21)

The typical Eastern inheritance system decreed that the elder brother be given two-thirds of the estate when the father died, and the younger brother one-third. In view of the outspoken request (almost a demand) he put to Jesus, it is easy to assume that the speaker was the younger brother and wanted to break with the traditional pattern. His rashness in breaking into Jesus' discourse gives ample evidence of his own greed.

Instead of entering into the family squabble, Jesus took the opportunity to go to the heart of the matter. He exposed the questioner's basic weakness while expounding to the crowd a principle that all needed to hear.

"Be on your guard against all kinds of greed . . . " He began (vs. 15). Basically the term means to desire to have more than one already has; undue affection for material things; "the spirit that is always wanting more" (Barclay).

What's wrong with wanting material things or wanting the best you can get? Jesus says this attitude makes it too easy to think we can buy happiness—that a certain level of material well-being is all we need to have peace. Materialism can breed false contentment with ourselves and the world around us, to the point of forgetting any sort of heavenly value system. Life on the earth, right now, can become all that matters to us. We get involved in the challenge of building bigger barns and lose sight of the fact that eventually those barns will rust or rot; whatever we have stored in them will be passed on to others; and we will have to stand before the Lord empty-handed.

The parable Jesus told was about a person whom we might call a good man. He does not say this man came by his wealth illegally or immorally. In fact, he had been blessed by God with rich soil that produced good crops in abundance. And he had made a good profit on the crop. He had apparently worked hard for what he owned.

Certain telltale elements in the story give clues about his attitude. He gave God no credit for his success and he repeatedly used "my" to show who was in control of the crops, barns, grain, and goods (vss. 17, 18).

As far as he was concerned, with this last crop in, he had enough goods to keep him in style for the rest of his life. His intention was to relax, indulge himself and take a leisurely, early retirement. Luke's choice of wording echoes both the traditional Jewish assumption that a good person would be rewarded with gain and the Stoic philosophy (popular in the culture of his readers) that there is no afterlife, so we should enjoy what we have while it lasts.

Since Luke is the only gospel writer to give us this story, he may have thought that the pull of riches was a particular problem in the second generation (about 70 A.D.) of the early church. Jesus' attitude is in sharp contrast with the later leaders of the Maccabeans, begun as a purely religious movement, who became preoccupied with power and riches during the years between Jesus' resurrection and Luke's writing the gospel. According to J. Massyngbaerd Ford (*My Enemy Is My Guest*), there may have been a fear that Christianity would deteriorate in the same way, leading to the many warnings about riches throughout the New Testament.

The Watcher (12:35-40)

The picture Jesus drew in this parable was of a master of a house who went off to a wedding and stayed much later than his servant's expected him to—somewhere between midnight and six a.m.—when it would be difficult for the servant to stay awake and watch. But a good servant's task was to do just that: to be awake when the master knocked.

Neither should a good servant scurry around trying to light the lamps, open the door, all the while tripping over a long-flowing robe in his haste. No, the good servant tucked up the long robe, worn in those days and still seen often in the Middle East, into his belt so he could work efficiently. He lit the lamps and kept them trimmed and burning and listened for the sound of the master's footsteps, no matter how late it was. Yawn! It would have been easy for the servant to doze off—weary with watching, discouraged, distracted by other things.

If the servants remained attentive to their primary responsibility—living so that nothing interfered with the master's return—then the master "will dress himself to serve, will have them recline at the table and will come and wait on them" (vs. 37). The lord of the house would honor the servants and share his own table with them, serving the meal. In the long run, the reward for faithfulness would be worth the effort of single-mindedness. We see that the reward is not riches, but a relationship with the Lord Himself!

Note that Jesus said that the master "will dress himself to serve" (vs. 37). "In antiquity, clothing was a manifestation, even an extension, of one's personality. Hence Jesus' teaching and action is highly challenging. The concept of the Son of Man serving others must have been astonishing, almost unbelievable, to the disciples" (Ford). In Luke 22:27 Jesus said, ". . . I am among you as one who serves."

In verse 39 there is a short parable that reinforces the need to be alert and faithful by adding contrast to the total picture. Like the servant, the householder was caught unprepared, perhaps distracted by other pursuits. Jesus ties the two together by saying, "You must be ready . . ." (vs. 40).

In the Parable of the Rich Fool and in the parables of the master who serves the watchful servants, Jesus again reverses the usual expectation of the day—that "goodness," as the Pharisees defined it, would lead to riches and that the Messiah would be easily recognized by His political power. Instead, the Kingdom consists in knowing God richly. The Messiah came without warning, to save by serving.

For Discussion

1. Jesus says a person's life does not consist in the abundance of his or her possessions. Yet, what are some ways we often define a person in terms of possessions?

2. What are some ways we can make ourselves "rich toward God"?

3. What practical steps can we take to break out of the mold of materialism that society tries to impose on us? How would you apply Luke 12:33?

Window on the Word

Two comments on the rich fool:

St. Augustine: "God desires not that thou shouldst lose thy riches, but that thou shouldst change their place."

St. Ambrose: "Thou hast barns—the bosoms of the needy, the houses of the widows, the mouths of orphans and infants."

8

Teaching About Lostness

Truth to Apply: God celebrates when His lost children are found.

Key Verse: "For this son of mine was dead and is alive again; he was lost and is found." So they began to celebrate (Lk. 15:24).

Oscar was a loser. The young bilingual man, who had left his native county after an argument with his family, had been in a car accident and had suffered some brain damage, which affected his memory from time to time. Because of this, his wife divorced him. He tried to commit suicide four times. Then he started attending a church where the people truly showed him love. He was converted and, as a Christian, became a changed man. Through the power of Christ, he became peaceful and better able to overcome his disabilities. He was eager to grow, hungry to learn Scripture, and sincerely sought God's ways.

Anna had come from the Middle East to study in a California college. One night a drunken business executive and his girl friend crashed into her car. The impact shattered Anna's face like a porcelain vase. Even after plastic surgery her own mother did not recognize her. After the accident (in which the guilty party was never charged) Anna had trouble concentrating in her studies and did so poorly that she was threatened with a loss of her student visa. Anna did not, so far as we know, yield her misfortune to Jesus Christ. But suppose she had. What changes might Christ have made in her life?

Parables comprise more than one-third of the recorded teachings of Jesus. (When asked a question, he usually asked a question in return or told a story.) Different scholars have suggested that Jesus told as few as 30 parables, or as many as around 80, depending on how *parable* is defined. David Redding asks, "What is a parable? A fable is a fantastic tale with trees and foxes speaking. A proverb is a statement with no tale at all. An allegory is a story with each part robotlike, standing for something. But a parable is a story true to this house of earth, but with a window open to the sky" (*Parables He Told, vii*).

Here are five clues to the characteristics of Jesus' parables:

1. They appear at first to be stories about everyday life but then turn out to be truths about God and his Kingdom.

2. They arouse curiosity and provoke the conscience.

3. They carry comparisons. A thing is *like* something else ("The kingdom of heaven is like . . . " Mt. 13:31).

4. They concentrate on one main point. That is not to say that only one feature in a parable may have meaning, but it guards against over embroidering every speck with significance.

5. The context often carries the explanation of, or clues to, a parable's meaning.

The major truth of the parable of the prodigal son is that this is a story of *God's* unlimited love for us. Few stories make us feel as good clear down to our toes as this one. The happy ending is a surprise to anyone who has ever run away from God or from responsibility. It is also a surprise to anyone who stayed home and thought they were being "responsible." It must have been a shock to the Pharisees, who objected to Jesus' activities (vs. 2).

Light on the Text

Glamourville Becomes Hog Trough (15:11-16)

This parable is the climax in a series on three (the lost sheep, the lost coin, and the lost son). The common denominators in the three parables in Luke 15 are that what was lost was found and that the finding brought joy to the seeker. These are the clues for interpreting this parable. Note also the progression not only in percentages (from 1 to 10 to 50 percent) but in value (from animate and inanimate items to a human being, a son). I. H. Marshall claims that "the younger" son (vs. 12) "may well have been about 17 years or more, since the story implies that he was unmarried (marriage took place normally at about 18-20 years . . .)" (*Commentary on Luke*). If you are a parent, you might think about what you would feel if your youngest child, at that age, made such a request of you. "Would you choose to have a ventriloquist's doll, or a child who may break your heart?" (J. Stafford Wright, *Man in the Process of Time*).

The son's request of verse 12 must be set within the context of ancient Jewish inheritance customs. Deuteronomy 21:17 indicates that "the firstborn" was to receive a "double share." Norvel Geldenhuys elaborates: "At that time the custom prevailed among the Jews that a father could either bequeath his possessions to his heirs by drawing up a testament or could even during his lifetime assign them to his heirs in the form of presents. As a rule, however. . . the father, although he had allotted to each son his share, still retained the . . . [legal use] of it until his death" (*Commentary on the Gospel of Luke*).

The son's footloose itch quickly took him away from home. Winston Churchill's novel *A Far Country* hints at the connections between spiritual and physical geography. The son not only left his father's home, but also left his values behind. He perhaps had in mind the possibility of making a much greater fortune in one of the big cities where he could find other Jews engaged in business.

There were many Jews outside the homeland, as Hendriksen states, probably about four million. In fact, E. M. Blaiklock observed that "Jews made up more than half the population of Alexandria, which, along with Rome, was one of the two most populous cities in the whole Mediterranean" (*Acts: The Birth of the Church*).

The results were tragic. He "squandered" (15:13) his wealth. (See Lk. 16:1, where the same word describes a manager who was accused of "wasting" another's possessions). Today young men and women also go to the big city seeking fame and fortune, only to waste what they have and to be broken by urban pressures. The city, which promises power and wealth, does not yield easily to fortune-seekers. In particular, those between the ages of 16 and 19 are the most vulnerable—just when they emerge from school, full of hope for their futures.

We are not told exactly how the younger brother squandered his wealth, but his older brother assumed that prostitutes were involved (vs. 30). At any rate, his resources came to an end, just as the country was suffering a famine, and he took work that must have shamed him. Jews did not keep pigs, considered unclean by the rabbis (see Lev. 11:7). "Cursed be the man who raises pigs, and cursed be the man who teaches his son Greek wisdom," they said.

The pods that had grown so appealing were from the carob tree. But these long sweet beans were usually only eaten by the poor. The parable begins with the son's request, "Father, give me my share . . . " and verse 16 concludes, "no one gave him anything."

Pigpen Becomes Think Tank (15:17-19)

Reflection (vs. 17), resolution (vs. 18a), repentance (vs. 18b), realization (vs. 19)—these are the steps to reception by the father (vs. 20ff). The pigpen became a place to think. It was there, in his desperation, that the son thought most clearly.

"He came to his senses . . . " A.T. Robertson says, "as if he had been as far from himself as he was from home." The same verb was also used medically, as when we say, "she came to." A similar expression is used for Peter waking up in Acts 12:11.

Like Augustine (c. A.D. 300) remembering his mother's prayers, or John Newton (c. 1750) recalling Mary Catlett back home, the young man in Luke 15:17 did not have a blank slate for a mind. Rather, his mental slate had indelibly etched upon it memories that said, "The grass was greener." His home life was a picture that called him to return.

Luke uses the term "hired men" to distinguish these workers from slaves. This means that his father probably was in the upper class, even more affluent than most slave owners.

The prodigal's resolve in verse 18 shows responsibility. There are no excuses at this point. He didn't blame his parents, the environment, the famine, poor working conditions, or his brother. He said, "I have sinned." He walked a long way on those words.

The Prodigal Father (15:20-24)

We do not know the father's age in the parable, but we have to admit that he had good vision and legs healthy enough for a mad dash down the road. ". . . Running was a most unusual and undignified thing for an aged Oriental to do" (J. Jeremias, *The Parables of Jesus*).

Then, in an action unfamiliar to most Western men, the father showered the son with kisses. The form of the Greek verb indicates that the father kissed him again and again. All this treatment was like a trumpet fanfare to the returnee.

One can imagine the boy's emotions. He probably felt like his voice was an echo chamber. But he choked out the rehearsed words—halfway. Jay Kessler says the definition of a father is someone who cuts a child off in the middle of a sentence. This father's overriding acceptance halted any proposals that the son become a hired man.

The father called for pomp and circumstance, for full dress regalia, for a welcome home party. He was prodigal in the best sense, "recklessly extravagant" (*Webster's New Collegiate Dictionary*). Both father and son in the story were free-fisted—the father with his love, the son with his living. (It would be interesting to speculate on other ways they were similar. Were they both fun-loving, friendly, party types? Why else would the father think of a feast for his returning son?)

The staccatolike commands began, "Bring the best robe" (vs. 22). Some scholars, claiming a literal translation for "best" and "first," contend that a former, treasured robe is taken out of storage, indicating a return to his old status. Perhaps the meaning is that the robe confers status. It was clearly a first-class robe, the house's finest. With the robe came a "ring," a word found only here in the New Testament. A. T. Robertson commented on the second and third items in the list: "Both sandals and rings are marks of the freeman as slaves were barefooted" (*Word Pictures in the New Testament, II*).

After his feet were shod, his food was prepared (vs.23). The *Wycliffe Bible Encyclopedia*, 1 states, "Calves were sometimes fattened in the stall (Amos 6:4; Mal. 4:2; Lk. 15:23) or kept around the house (I Sam. 28:24). They supplied veal (Gen. 18:7), which was considered a delicacy for the wealthy (Amos 6:4)."

A runaway rebel had returned. The result was rejoicing—"they began to celebrate." The father who had given the younger sons his premature inheritance was back at it again—giving, giving, and more giving! After all, ours is the God "who gives generously to all without finding fault" (Jas. 1:5).

For Discussion

1. Consider the members of your family or circle of friends who are like the younger son—free-fisted, generous, friendly, fun-loving. What could you do for them now that might prevent their becoming lost in the big city?

2. Where would you find the "losers," modern prodigals, within ten miles of your home address?

3. Lists three ways you or your church might better seek out and love these persons.

Window on the Word

Charles Trumbull met a drunk man on public transportation. The inebriate offered to share his drink with Trumbull, who replied, "Well, I can see you are a very generous man." From that point emerged a conversation in which Trumbull helped to lead the man to Christ. It was Trumbull's kind remark that opened Heaven's doors.

9

Teaching About Stewardship

Truth to Apply: Because the Kingdom is here, it is urgent that I be prudent and faithful to God in handling money.

Key Verse: No servant can serve two masters. Either he will hate the one and love the other, or he will be devoted to the one and despise the other. You cannot serve both God and Money (Lk. 16:13).

"A frantic pounding on our door interrupted the serenity of our first day on Maui, Hawaii. You've got to evacuate! the manager shouted. A *tsunami* is coming in one hour!

"I thought he was joking. I didn't even know what a *tsunami* was. I soon learned that it's a tidal wave.

"An earthquake of 7.7 magnitude had shaken the Aleutian Islands off Alaska, and its shock began a tidal wave that was rushing toward Hawaii, scheduled to arrive at 5:06 p.m. In the late 1800s a 100-foot tidal wave struck with tragic destruction. In 1957 a 40-foot wave rushed onto Kauai.

"Bitter experience taught the Islanders to treat such warnings with great respect. But what about us tourists? I didn't see how it could occur. The ocean appeared to be so calm. Yet I realized it could happen.

"So we grabbed a few items—a jacket, water, a Bible, another book, my peanut M&Ms!" (Jerry White, *Choosing Plan A in a Plan B World*).

According to the Scripture, Jesus will come with even less warning. What does it mean for you to be "ready"?

The chief character in this week's parable is a steward. In the early history of the English language a steward was a *stiweard* (from *sti*, meaning "hall," plus *weard*, meaning "ward") that is, someone charged with the care, for instance, of a pigsty. This narrower meaning sheds light upon the broader one—anyone in charge of anything.

There were three basic Hebrew expressions and two Greek ones representing steward in the Bible. The Greek word used in Luke 16 is *oikonomos*, from which we derive "economy." A steward was usually someone second in rank who exercised certain supervisory duties. The *Wycliffe Bible Encyclopedia* states, "The steward's duties usually included such responsibilities as the oversight of meals, household finances, servants, children of the family, flocks and herds, and tilling of the fields."

Some of the functions of stewards in the Bible may be seen by a sampling of passages. Abraham's steward was trusted with the responsibility of selecting a wife for Isaac (Gen. 24). Joseph, second in the land of Egypt, had a steward who functioned, among other things, as a door-keeper (Gen. 43:19). King David possessed stewards "over all the property and livestock belonging to the king and his sons" (I Chr. 28:1). In Luke we read of "Chuza, the manager of Herod's household" (8:3). In one of Jesus' parables, the steward pays the day laborers for their work (Mt. 20:8). Romans 16:23 mentions Erastus, the city's director (*oikonomos*) of public works, as among the believers.

The breadth of the word steward may be seen in the ways various versions translate it. The steward in Luke 16 is called an "accountant" in the Living Bible. J. B. Phillips calls him an "agent." The New English Bible prefers "manager," and Moffatt employs a less familiar British expression, "factor."

Light on the Text

Resolute Action in a Crisis (16:1-8)

In Luke 16 we have the colorful story about a rich landlord and a remarkable rogue who functioned as his business manager. (Note that Luke 16:19 begins another story with the same wording, "There was a rich man . . . .") Perhaps the rich were frequently absentee landlords, somewhat like the "man of noble birth [who] went to a distant country" (Lk. 19:12). If so, he needed a plantation manager to keep the farm running smoothly while he was off wheeling and dealing in cities like Damascus or Alexandria.

Both the prodigal son (15:13) and the wasteful steward (16:1) squandered their master's money. Both parables involve financial questions. The father with his estate (15:12) parallels the rich man (16:1). By contrast, the prodigal repented, while the steward did not. The three parables of Luke 15 were about tax collectors and sinners (15:1) in the presence of the Pharisees and the teachers of the Law (15:2), while the parable of the shrewd manager was about the Pharisees, but was told to Jesus' disciples (16:1).

The manager in this story functioned much as did Joseph for Pharaoh in Genesis 41:38-57. He was proprietor of the plantation, minister of finance, credit manager for the firm, etc. In short, he was in complete charge of the estate.

He was accused of wasting the master's resources and faced an audit and dismissal. Picture him stalking off into a corner to have a talk with himself: "I'm too unskilled to dig and I'm too proud to beg. What am I going to do?" There was no unemployment office to see and no unemployment check to draw!

"Ah, I know what I will do" is how the Jerusalem Bible renders the opening of Luke 16:4. "I know just the thing!" the Living Bible has it. The quick thinking business agent had arrived at a swift verdict, showing foresight for those days ahead when he would be discharged from his duties. He faced an overwhelming problem and acted decisively.

Luke 16:5-7 gives the gist of the conference called by this shrewd employee. He held a conference with the persons who owed his boss money. Probably, in Middle Eastern fashion, their contract was verbal and had been arranged through the same steward.

He told them that their I.O.U.'s were to be altered. Debtor #1 owed 800 gallons of olive oil. His debt was cut in half. No doubt the wheat farmer brightened up after seeing this. He owed 1,000 bushels, which was reduced to 800. The job was quickly done. He had guaranteed himself a reception in their homes when he would lose his job.

As verse 8a suggests, the story is a summons to resolute action in a crisis (J. Jeremias, *The Parables of Jesus*). The steward is commended only for his prudence, a kind of "non-moral cleverness and skill deployed in self-preservation" (*Theological Dictionary of the New Testament, Vol VII*, p. 484).

"Even now the axe is laid to the root of the trees . . . ." (Lk. 3:9). As Jesus speaks to His disciples, He is also aiming a barb at the eaves-dropping Pharisees. Jeremias sums it up: "You are in the same position as this steward who saw the imminent disaster threatening him with ruin, but the crisis which threatens you, in which, indeed, you are already involved, is incomparably more terrible....the challenge of the hour demands prudence, everything is at stake" (*The Parables of Jesus*).

The Moral in an Immoral Action (16:9-13)

The Pharisees and scribes (Lk. 15:2) treated humans contemptuously, and money covetously (Lk. 16:14). Instead of using things and loving people, they had a "keep out" policy toward people and a "keep it" policy toward money. As Luke surveyed the Church in 70 A.D., when he wrote, he saw a similar temptation and used several of Jesus' own comments (perhaps spoken originally in other contexts) as a way of applying the parable also to their need to act prudently in dealing with money.

First, he says, "Use worldly wealth to gain friends;" in other words, use it properly; use money to serve people. Friendship is sometimes a forgotten art among us, due to the money orientation of our culture. Young urban professionals are urged by advertising to "have it all," meaning cars, gourmet food, houses, vacations. There is little room for friends in the deep sense of the word. Friendship itself has become a tool for professional and financial advancement. Jesus says, put it the other way round. Use money to deepen friendship, rather than using friendship to make money.

At the corporate level, a similar subordination of people to money occurs. Some operators go through a string of bankruptcies, putting people out of work and ruining investors, but always driving away in their fine cars. Corporations become more interested in the survival of their identities, cutting quality or selling off divisions to get cash, with little thought for the customer who is affected by shoddy goods or the worker pained by the turmoil of restructuring.

In verses 10-12 we have several maxims on money, partly to prevent any misunderstanding of the morality in the parable and partly to apply the main point to our stewardship. Verse 10 verifies that the one who can be trusted with a little can be trusted with a lot.

In verse 11 the meaning of 10 is amplified. The "very little" and the "much" are explained in terms of "worldly wealth" and "true riches." *The Interpreter's Bible* illustrates this well: "Imagine a woodcarver testing his son's skill. He would use clay, not fine oak. If the boy showed promise with a base medium, the father would then let him try his hand with fine wood. That is why money is important—as training ground for real living" (vol. 8, p. 286). Verse 12 implies that everything we have is on loan from the Lord ("someone else's property").

The wrap-up of the parable's application is found in verse 13. The verse implies that if we don't master money, money will master us. In the final analysis, we cannot have divided devotion. Paul commented that "greed . . . is idolatry" (Col. 3:5).

It has been said that "God will not share the throne in our lives with any other. He requires a single-minded life. He will not settle for a divided service." In Galatians 1:10, Paul wrote, "If I were still trying to please men, I would not be a servant of Christ."

"No servant can serve two masters. Either he will hate the one and love the other, or he will be devoted to the one and despise the other. You cannot serve both God and Money" (vs. 13). These words are also found in the Sermon on the Mount (Mt. 6:24), where they are set in the context of caring about God rather than material things. Here in Luke they are framed in the urgency of the arrival of the Kingdom and the necessity to use things wisely. Jesus said that the wisest thing, the urgent thing to do with money is not to become devoted to it, as the Pharisees were (vs. 14).

For Discussion

1. If a person had more money, do you think he or she

would be essentially more generous with it? Support your answer.

2. How can people be helped and influenced for good through the wise use of money? Or, how can you deepen a friendship through the wise use of money?

3. What do you think the Church needs to do to meet more adequately its stewardship mission in our day?

Window on the Word

Dr. Haddon Robinson, president of Denver Seminary, tells about the story (told by Sigmund Freud) about a sailor who was washed ashore on a Pacific island. The natives made him king of the island. However, as he came to understand their language and customs, he found that he was to be king for a year and then left to starve to death on a nearby island.

The sailor-become-king sent some servants over to the second island to till the soil. Later he commanded them to put seeds in the plowed ground. Still later, he ordered his favorite items taken over to that island. As a result, when his fateful time came, instead of going to a place of death he was taken to a place of prosperity.

"It is a truism," says Dr. Robinson, "that you can't take it with you. But it is a truth of heaven that by shrewd investment we can send something valuable on ahead."

10

Going Up to Jerusalem

Truth to Apply: Jesus' presence is my personal invitation to celebrate, and also provides a challenge for me to live a life-style of purity.

Key Verse: As the time approached for him to be taken up to heaven, Jesus resolutely set out for Jerusalem (Lk. 9:51).

The Jewish Temple was at the spiritual center of Jerusalem. The city itself stood on a hill, so the most prominent landmark visible from a distance was the gleaming Temple. It was where God was worshiped. There at one time the Ark of the Covenant had rested. To the Temple every Jewish man traveled at least once in life, no matter how far away He lived.

When Jesus came, He expanded the concept of the temple to mean one's bodily life. His death and resurrection made our bodies temples of the Holy Spirit (I Cor. 6:19, 20). "Don't you know," Paul asks, "that you yourselves are God's temple and that God's Spirit lives in you? If anyone destroys God's temple, God will destroy him; for God's temple is sacred and you are that temple" (I Cor. 3:16, 17).

What happens when Christ the Lord and King comes into our temple, which is also His house? What will He see that needs cleaning out?

After describing the circumstances of Jesus' birth and His early teaching and healing ministry, Luke ends the first third of his gospel with the words, "As the time approached for him to be taken up to heaven, Jesus resolutely set out for Jerusalem" (Lk. 9:51). This is, you will note, the Bible verse at the head of this chapter.

From his account of the Transfiguration onward, Luke portrays every act and word of Jesus from the standpoint of His self-knowledge of His Messiahship and the sacrificial death that would demand. In this context, therefore, Luke relates Jesus' subsequent parables and acts of healing. With every word and deed, He was drawing closer to the foreseen conclusion of His ministry.

As He drew near Jerusalem (Lk. 19:11-27), Jesus told His disciples a parable to help them understand the true nature of the Kingdom of God and how it was to come to fulfillment. The disciples did not, at the time, understand what He was saying or make the correct application, but later they came to accept His words as both a warning and a comfort.

After His explanation, Jesus *went on ahead*, completing the journey toward Jerusalem to which Luke referred ten chapters earlier. The phrase "going up to Jerusalem" (an echo of 9:51) implies Jesus' knowledge of who He was. His was not a slowly unfolding revelation but an acceptance of a role and mission of which He was fully aware. Jesus knew He was fulfilling prophecy, and His words were designed to explain God's love to those who heard Him. His acts of healing were not only demonstrations of His love and compassion but were also validations of His message.

Light on the Text

The King with a Plan (19:29-34)

Bethphage, some Bible scholars suggest, was a suburb of Bethany, the home of Mary, Martha, and Lazarus. Bethany was just a couple of miles from Jerusalem on the slope of the Mount of Olives. It was the village just ahead of them (vs. 30).

Some commentators suggest "the Lord needs it" was a previously established password. Others suggest that the interaction shows that the owners of the colt were followers of Jesus and the fact that "the Lord needs it" was sufficient reason to allow the disciples to take the animal.

Whichever way one may interpret the conversation, it is certainly clear that Jesus not only was working from a predetermined plan but chose a colt to ride because of His awareness of Old Testament prophecy. It also points to the way Jesus chooses to work, even today.

We, too, are needed by the Lord. It is His chosen way of working. We enter into the Jerusalem (centers of power) of our day with Him to do His work and His will. No Christian should ever forget the importance of faithfulness in small things. Like the disciples, we should be ready at any time to obey Christ's every command.

Celebration and Worship (19:35-40)

The disciples in the first two verses of the preceding section were very likely the twelve, plus others of Jesus' most faithful followers. John tells us (Jn. 11) that as a result of the raising of Lazarus from the dead shortly before Jesus entered Jerusalem, many new followers were attracted to Jesus and continued with Him after that event.

Because it was Passover week, Jews throughout the countryside and from neighboring lands had gathered in Jerusalem. Many of these had heard of Jesus; many had seen His miracles and heard His teaching. Running through the mind and heart of most every Jew was the desire for the Savior-King to come. The common understanding of His role, however, was that He would come as a conquering warrior, ready to overthrow the hated Roman rule and restore Jerusalem to its rightful owners.

As word spread that Jesus was approaching from the Mount of Olives, surrounded by a throng of disciples, more and more Jews from around the Temple left the place of worship to join the welcoming multitudes. They threw their cloaks into the path in front of Jesus, thereby acknowledging His Kingship in a traditional Eastern response. In II Kings 9:13 we read about garments being placed at the feet of Jehu as He was proclaimed king.

Jesus' entry into Jerusalem on a donkey was foretold in Zechariah 9:9: "Rejoice greatly, O Daughter of Zion! Shout,

65

daughter of Jerusalem! See, your king comes to you, righteous and having salvation, gentle and riding on a donkey, on a colt, the foal of a donkey." Many of the prophecies Jesus fulfilled during His earthly ministry, especially those connected with the last week before the Cross, were not understood by the disciples until after His resurrection. Many prophecies had to be explained to them by Jesus Himself, as, for example, in His conversation with the two on the road to Emmaus (Lk. 24).

It is important to realize that while there was certainly an emotional element in this celebration parade (as with any joyful occasion), this was not merely a thrill-seeking crowd that found a diversion or a good show. Some of the people were there praising Jesus and worshiping Him as having come from God because they had heard His teaching and had been present as He healed the sick and raised the dead. Being stirred to praise and worship by valid firsthand experience is not the same as allowing oneself to be carried away by the emotion of crowd psychology.

The cry of joy, "Blessed is the king who comes in the name of the Lord!" is an echo of Psalm 118:26. Recognizing Jesus' mission, the crowd spontaneously sang their praise in the words of Scripture.

Enter the Pharisees. We might ask why the Pharisees were there anyway. The most obvious answer is that they wanted to keep a watchful eye on a potential troublemaker. John reports that after Jesus raised Lazarus from the dead, the Pharisees and chief priests and scribes got together to discuss the matter. They were afraid that if Jesus continued His activities, so much attention would be drawn to Him that the Romans would become concerned.

Some commentators suggest that even up until this time some of the Pharisees were interested in Jesus' message and were following along in order to hear His words and evaluate for themselves the truth of what He preached. Whether they were critics or truth seekers, the Pharisees in the crowd were shocked by the honor the people accorded Jesus. Most likely they recognized enough Scriptural allusions in the shouts of the crowd and Jesus' remarks to believe they had grounds on which to accuse Him of blasphemy and heresy.

They demanded that Jesus rebuke and quiet the crowd. When they addressed Him, they used the word "teacher"—a safe term, devoid of any sense of divinity. They apparently were careful not to give Him even the status of a prophet. They wanted to make their stand concerning His religious authority quite clear.

Jesus' response indicated that a power so great was at work in their situation that if all the people were to be mute, even stones would break forth in praise. This was the final blow to the Pharisee's patience. We hear no more of them until we find them plotting to have Jesus arrested and killed.

The King Exhibits His Authority (19:45-48)

We need to go to the other gospel accounts to learn that on that first day, Jesus entered the Temple, sized up the situation and returned to Bethany for the night. The following day, He came back to the Temple and the encounter with the money changers took place.

By expelling from the Temple the money changers and the sellers of animal and cereal sacrifices that the Law required, Jesus asserted His authority. In entering the Temple, He had returned home. "My house," He said, quoting Scripture, "is the house of prayer." Scripture does not record how the Temple leaders and money changers reacted to His anger. No overt action was taken against Him. Perhaps, in spite of themselves, they recognized the righteousness in what He did; probably they had to admit grudgingly that He was right.

The area of the Temple in which the buying and selling took place was the outer court, the Court of the Gentiles. The area was as close to the Holy Place as a non-Jew could come in order to worship Yahweh. The Scripture Jesus quoted to the money changers is the last phrase from Isaiah 56:6, 7, which begins "foreigners who bind themselves to the Lord to serve Him," whom God "will bring to . . . [His] house of prayer."

In His action Jesus claimed divine authority (see Mt. 12:6) and His sense of the holiness of the Temple area. He also hinted that God would call Gentiles as well as Jews to Himself.

Each night Jesus and His disciples returned to Bethany and each day they came back to the Temple where He taught large crowds. He presented an understanding of God that the common people had not heard before. "All the people hung on His words" (vs. 48) and the chief priests and scribes could not find a way to kill Him.

For Discussion

1. How are the opening moments of a worship service like the entry of Jesus into Jerusalem? What feelings and responses are appropriate?

2. Take a look at the order of worship (printed in your church bulletin) and identify those items that point to Jesus' presence and those in which we respond to Him.

3. What changes in the service would make it easier for you to celebrate Jesus' presence?

4. The next time you are in a worship service, meditate on Psalm 24 or 118:19-29 beforehand. Afterward, ask yourself: "How did this change my ability to celebrate?"

Window on the Word

"Now Jesus returns to the Temple. What is to be done with it—the old inherited religion of His people? What happens to men's beliefs and ideas when Jesus comes to inspect them?

"Jesus comes to cast a critical eye over what the Jews have made of their very special relationship with God. He finds much that needs cleaning up, much grime and rubbish that needs removing . . . .

"The evils which had accumulated in Judaism in the time of Jesus are not peculiar to the Jerusalem Temple. We may all find, as Jesus enters our own temple and inspects our faith and life, things that need to be thoroughly cleaned out from it."

(Michael Wilcock, *Savior of the World: The Message of Luke's Gospel*, InterVarsity Press)

11

Observing the Last Supper

Truth to Apply: My holy celebration—past, present, and future—is focused on Jesus Christ.

Key Verse: And he took bread, gave thanks and broke it, and gave it to them, saying, "This is my body given for you; do this in remembrance of me" (Lk. 22:19).

What thoughts come to your mind when you take part in a Communion service?

One woman responded, "In my childhood, church was a place where you dare not even so much as smile, or Mom would rap your knuckles. And Communion was most somber. I can remember thinking like I felt as though I was at a funeral."

A man who remembers his days in the Air Force, when he served overseas, said, "As I sit quietly meditating and preparing to receive the bread and the cup, I sometimes think of the fact that all over the world there are people having Communion like me. And I get a feeling of excitement, realizing that I'm a member of a great big family of people who have found new life through Jesus Christ."

Or, you might be like the person who remembers the service as "a Eucharist, a thanksgiving in a big old downtown church. The congregation was a mix of stockbrokers, street people, musicians, nurses and secretaries; single people and families; blacks and whites. The organ and choir provided a musical setting, parts of the liturgy were sung and along with the people I thought about the great feast to which we are invited someday, the marriage supper of the Lamb."

What do you think about during the Lord's Supper?

Background/Overview: *Luke 22:1-23*

This chapter reaches a climax in the beloved physician's account of the completion of Jesus' earthly ministry. Like the writers of the other gospel accounts, Luke devotes considerable space to the events of the passion.

See the outline of Luke below and notice the number of chapters devoted to each period of time. Five and a half chapters are devoted to the last week of Jesus' life, compared to three and a half chapters for the first 30 years. (The last four verses of the gospel happened 40 days after the resurrection, but otherwise the section from 19:28—24:49 took one week).

Preparation near the city	Ministry in the cities	Journey to the city	Accomplishment in the city
1:1 4:13	4:14 9:50	9:51 18:30	18:31 24
30 years	2 1/2 years	6 months	1 week

19:28   That day before the crucifixion was very full. There is almost a breathlessness in Luke's telling it, as though he feels the weight of happening upon happening crying out to be told.

In chapter 22, Luke presents the events that took place in the evening and the greater part of the night. But the night gives way to dawn, a day that did not bring relief to Jesus but, rather, spread out in its glare the ugliness of death and taunting crowds.

Light on the Text

Passover Politics (22:1, 2)

The Passover festivities, one of the peaks of Jewish religious celebration, occurs each year in March or April at the time of the spring full moon. It was also the first of eight days of the Feast of Unleavened Bread, an agricultural festival related to beginning of the spring barley harvest. In Palestine, seeding occurs during the months of November and December, and harvesting between April and June. The Feast of Pentecost occurred 50 days after Passover, during which the first harvest sheaves were presented to

God in the Temple at Jerusalem, marking the end of the grain harvest.

The Passover and the Feast of Unleavened Bread had come to be so closely associated that Luke could merge them for his largely Gentile readership. Strictly speaking, however, Passover began on the 14th day of the Jewish month of Nisan at sundown and the Feast of Unleavened Bread began on the 15th and lasted until the 21st. In a solemn ceremony on the evening of the 13th of Nisan, household heads lit candles and meticulously searched their houses to ensure that no trace of unleavened bread remained in the home.

According to Jewish Law, every Jewish male who lived within 15 miles of the city was required to be at the feast. Many who lived far beyond that limit cherished the thought of being at the festival, and many of them came from other nations around the Mediterranean. Understandably, the population of Jerusalem swelled enormously during the feast days. Homeowners were expected to house pilgrims without charge. In one year during the first century, 256,000 lambs were slain for the sacrifices, one for each family or group of friends.

As Jesus moved among the swirling throngs and taught in the Temple, the priests did not feel they could send soldiers to capture Him by force without risking a riot, for which they would have to answer to the Roman overlords. Jesus' heterodoxy, as they considered it, His razor-sharp attack on hypocrisy and the possibility that the Romans might regard His popularity as a source of trouble, confirmed their resolve to end His life somehow—as they had ended the lives of so many other lambs.

Passover Preparations (22:7-13)

The Passover lambs were traditionally killed in the Court of the Priests in the Temple area. The actual slaying took place between about 2:30 and 5:30 on the afternoon of the 14th of Nisan. The head of each family did the slaughtering, while a priest caught the animal's blood in a bowl and poured it at the foot of the altar of burnt offering. Families then purchased unleavened bread, bitter herbs and wine, and went home to roast the lamb.

Jesus said to Peter and John, "Go and prepare us the passover" (vs. 8). He was asking them to purchase and

71

sacrifice a lamb, buy the bread, herbs and wine, and then cook the lamb in an oven. Perhaps because He was aware of the traitorous activities of Judas, Jesus had made plans for the celebration of His last supper on earth without even consulting His closest disciples. They had to ask where He would like them to prepare the meal.

Since carrying water jars was normally the work of women or slaves, it appears that the man was not a slave and that he was a prearranged sign for Peter and John. The water probably was for washing the celebrant's hands prior to eating the Passover meal. Jesus told Peter and John to say to the owner of the house, "The Teacher asks . . ." implying that he was not only a friend but also a follower/student of Jesus.

The guest room of verse 11 could have been the large main room on the ground floor of the home. The upper room (verse 12) was the best room of the house, one reserved only for special guests. Most houses, especially those of the more well-to-do, were two stories high with a flat roof. Lamb and other foods could be prepared in the courtyard. Animals and slaves lived on the lower level. The family occupied the upper level. On hot nights, however they would sleep on the roof, which was also used to dry food in the sun.

Passover Proceedings (22:14-20)

At the very last possible moment, Jesus told the other apostles, including Judas, where they would be eating the meal. In that way Judas had no immediate opportunity to make contact with those who were plotting Jesus' death. That would come later.

Imagine a group of men moving though the courtyard past the oven, where Peter and John had supervised the cooking of the lamb, and up the stairs to the guest room. Each of them would have washed his hands with the water brought to the house by the man Peter and John had met earlier. Later, perhaps from the same water, Jesus washed the feet of His friends and disciples (Jn. 13:2-5).

Our own mental picture of the scene may be that of 13 people sitting around our own dining room table. Or we might think of Leonardo da Vinci's famous painting of the last supper, which depicts Jesus seated at the middle of a long table covered with bread, rolls, wine glasses or cups, and flat empty plates—flanked on each side by six disciples, with Judas listening to Peter as he whispered in John's ear (Jn. 13:24).

These pictures, however, reflect the eating practices of the 15th or 20th centuries, not first-century Palestine. The text says they "reclined at table" (Lk. 22:14). In those times, the tables were low. Servants served from one side and the guests reclined on couches around the other three sides with their heads close to the table, their left elbows propped up on cushions.

Jesus says, "I have eagerly desired to eat . . ." (vs. 15), more literally "with desire I have desired." Luke uses repetitive phrases like this, more typical of Hebrew, to emphasize the intensity of the emotions. The pace is quickening. The goal is in sight. Jesus came to die and this is one of the last steps on the way to His fulfillment.

The word "again" in verse 16 implies that Jesus would not eat bread or drink wine again until He returned at the end of the age. He would soon fulfill the Passover for all time. At the coming future Kingdom, "he will renew fellowship with those who through the ages have commemorated the Lord's Supper . . . in the great Messianic 'wedding supper' to come (Rev. 19:9)" (*The NIV Study Bible*, p. 1582).

During a Jewish Passover, four or five cups of wine were handed around. The head of the household began the repast with a blessing of the first cup that may, even in Jesus' day, have already included the words, "Blessed be Thou, O Lord our God, the King of the world, who hast created the fruit of the vine." If so, Jesus, in verse 18, may have alluded to that prayer.

The cup after the supper (vs. 20) may have been the last cup. If so, it would have followed the eating of the bitter herbs, an explanation of the meaning of Passover, eating the lamb and unleavened cakes. Each item had a highly developed symbolic meaning. *Haroset*, for example, a finely chopped mixture of apples, nuts, raisins, cinnamon and wine, symbolizes the mortar the Israelites used to make bricks in Egypt.

Another element in the meal was the singing of Psalms 113–118. These formed the "Egyptian Hallel," used at the Feasts of Passover, Weeks, Tabernacles, Dedication and New Moon. At Passover, Psalms 113 and 114 were sung before the meal, and Psalms 115–118 after the meal (*The NIV Study Bible*, p. 908).

For Discussion

1. If you had been present at the Last Supper, what might have been your dominant emotion?

2. How can the Lord's Supper become a more meaningful celebration for you?

3. What suggestions do you have for improving the celebration of the Lord's Supper at your church?

Window on the Word

Making Bread for a Jewish Passover Seder

"Matzah is baked quickly, taking no more than eighteen minutes from beginning to end, in a room shielded from sunlight. Counters and rollers are sanded smooth to prevent the dough from being contaminated by a piece of dough from an earlier baking. The dough is rolled and pricked continuously to prevent rising. The water used must be cool and preferably drawn from a well, at twilight the evening before, to stand throughout the night. The water cannot be used before daylight, but no rays of the sun may fall on it. No salt may be added to the matzah. The fire to bake the matzah ideally is started with willow branches saved from the Feast of Tabernacles, *Sukkoth*, the fall before."

(Ruth Gruber Fredman, *The Passover Seder*)

12

Suffering Crucifixion

Truth to Apply: Jesus saves me through His death.

Key Verse: Jesus called out with a loud voice, "Father, into your hands I commit my spirit." When he had said this, he breathed his last (Lk. 23:46).

Were you there when they crucified my Lord?
  Were you there when they crucified my Lord?
Oh! Sometimes it causes me to tremble, tremble, tremble.
  Were you there when they crucified my Lord?

Were you there when they nailed Him to the tree?
  Were you there when they nailed Him to the tree?
Oh! Sometimes it causes me to tremble, tremble, tremble.
  Were you there when they nailed Him to the tree?

Were you there when they pierced Him in the side?
  Were you there when they pierced Him in the side?
Oh! Sometimes it causes me to tremble, tremble, tremble.
  Were you there . . . .

How can I be there, when I'm here?

Background/Overview: *Luke 23*

The English word *crucifixion* comes from the Latin verb *crucifigere*, meaning "to fasten to a cross." Traditional pictures of a post thrust into the ground with a crosspiece to which the arms were nailed do not tell the whole story of this very brutal instrument of torture and death.

The earliest cross was a pointed stake, the kind used to build fences around ancient forts. Criminals in ancient Persia and Carthage were bound to such stakes. Scholars debate whether the Phenicians or Egyptians were the first to add the cross piece, called a *patibulum*, and to tie (or more often nail) the victim's hands to it to increase the length and severity of His suffering.

Crucifixion was not uniquely a Roman method of execution. Centuries earlier, King Darius of Persia crucified 3,000 political agitators. The notorious King Antiochus Epiphanes of Syria crucified many Jews who resisted his program of Hellenization. And about 88 B.C. one of the Jewish kings of the Maccabean dynasty crucified 800 Pharisees.

Notice the people surrounding the Crucifixion: the two criminals, the onlooking crowd, the soldiers, the rulers. Every element in human life is represented—criminal, military, religious, working class. Notice, too, the sounds of the Crucifixion: the hammer blows, the grunts of the solders lifting the cross into its socket, the shouts, the mocking, the forgiving words of Jesus, the last cry to the Father. The entire scene is a singularly odd blend of pathos and apathy—the caring Christ and the jeering mob. Even the sign over the cross is strangely mixed: printed in three languages, one for each of the major cultures of the day.

Yet not one thing was out of place. The great and awful drama of salvation's purchase came about exactly as foretold. Salvation is of the Lord.

Light on the Text

Condemnation (23:32, 33)

The simple majesty of God's Word is sometimes awesome. "They crucified him." In three short, clear words, the key event toward which this Gospel has moved is recorded.

After all the previous words, the economy here is striking.

Michael Wilcock (*Savior of the World*) points out that the distance from the judgment hall to the place of crucifixion is just a few hundred yards. "But the road to the cross is a long, long one measured in time. We can trace it, and see the cross at the end of it, through the whole of Luke's Gospel." He mentions 2:34, 35 (Simeon), 9:22; 13:32, 33; 17:25; and 18:31-33 (Jesus' predictions of His death), plus 9:31 (Moses and Elijah discussing Jesus' "departure" with Him) as way stations to the cross.

Only those who were not Roman citizens were subjected to the indignities of crucifixion. Death did not occur through loss of blood, from the nailed hands and feet, but through exhaustion and, as the body slumped and the fastened arms pulled against the chest, suffocation.

The Greek word, sometimes translated "Calvary" here, is *cranion*, meaning a skull. The word "calvary" comes from the Latin Vulgate translation made by Jerome between 383 and 405. Almost all modern translations substitute the phrase "the place called the Skull" (Lk. 23:33). It probably referred to a geographical formation that looked like a skull.

Mockery (23:34-38)

It is often difficult for us to forgive even the small and usually unintentional slights of others. Sometimes our church membership lists are peppered with the names of people who used to be active—until the pastor or some other church member said something that offended. Years, even decades, go by and nothing anyone can say or do seems to enable them to forgive.

Yet in the midst of His suffering, Jesus forgave. Instead of complaining about what others did to Him, instead of thinking about His own agony, Jesus in His customary way thought about the spiritual welfare of those who needed to be forgiven.

When Jesus said "forgive them," who is meant? It is hard to tell. According to a strict application of the rules of grammar, the criminals would be the objects of God's forgiveness. More likely, however, Jesus was referring to the Romans He could see around the cross. Or He might even have been thinking of the religious leaders, who thought they knew what they were doing but in fact had a very pinched view of their faith and Jesus' relationship to it.

The reference to dividing up and casting lots for Jesus' clothes (vs. 34) is a fulfillment of Psalm 22:18. The whole Psalm should be read for background when studying the Crucifixion because there are so many references to it in the narrative. Jesus seems to have been meditating on it as He hung on the cross and Luke also has it in mind as he describes the crowd and the soldiers in verses 35 and 36 (see Ps. 22:7, 17).

Jewish males usually wore two garments. Although Luke does not tell us exactly what Jesus had been wearing, John 19:23 tells us the soldiers took His clothes, i.e., the square piece of cloth thrown over one or both shoulders that was used as a sheet at night, and divided it into four shares. Then they cast lots for the seamless undergarment, the linen or wool shirt worn next to the skin and covering the body to the knees or ankles.

Some have seen in Luke's description of the people around the cross four basic types of abuse to which Jesus was subjected. First, the people "stood watching" (vs. 35). To them, a crucifixion was a spectacle to be stared at, much as people today rush to the scene of an accident to gawk. Even more open hostility is implied in the sneering of the rulers, the mocking of the soldiers, and the insults of one of the criminals.

Vinegar may seem like a strange beverage for the soldiers to offer Jesus. It was a cheap, sour wine that was carried by soldiers of that day and more effective in quenching thirst than water. They seem to be offering it in jest here, during the morning. John records that He did drink some, later that afternoon, when He cried out in thirst (Jn. 19:28-30).

The superscription mentioned in verse 38 was on a placard, a board painted white with gypsum that the Romans called a *titulus*. They may have hung it around Jesus' neck when, in the Praetorium, they mockingly saluted Him as King of the Jews (Mk. 15:16-20). Condemned criminals usually wore the *titulus* around the neck, though it was sometimes nailed to the cross. Normally the criminals' name and illegal activity were inscribed on it for everyone to read. Since Luke does not mention the wording until the end of his account, he probably intended us to understand it as the ultimate of the abuses of Jesus, and an ironic one because it was true. Jesus is the King of the Jews—and of all people.

Remembrance (23:39-43)

The two criminals contrast the two types of people in the world: the repentant and the self-righteous. Luke tells us that one asked to be remembered in the Kingdom, which Matthew and Mark omit. Perhaps his careful investigation turned up the story. It also fits with his interest in the variety of people who were drawn to Christ.

The repentant robber's (Mark's term for those crucified with Jesus) words are unusual. You don't ordinarily ask a dying man to remember you when He comes into His kingdom. The language suggests that he may have at some earlier point heard Jesus talk about the Kingdom.

Jesus told the penitent he would be with Him in "paradise." This word is one of the few English words that came to us from a Greek-Iranian origin. It literally means "an enclosed park." Jews believed in a shadowy afterlife in *sheol*, often just translated "the grave." Also, they later believed that a special felicity awaited the righteous. The penitent thief was rewarded with more than he asked for: a joyful life with Jesus in Paradise—not at some distant time, but *now*—"today."

The End (23:44-46)

Mark tells us that Jesus was crucified at the third hour (9 a.m.). Luke does not mention the time of the Crucifixion, but he does mention a spectacular darkness from the sixth hour (noon) until the ninth hour (3 p.m.).

Some scholars point out that Luke's description is astronomically impossible, that a solar eclipse is impossible at the time of a full moon, such as always occurred at Passover. Others, who insist that the sun was literally darkened, argue for a special, supernatural act of God that darkened the sun temporarily. Still others, aware that an eclipse of the sun was part of the imagery associated with the Day of the Lord in the Old Testament (Isa. 13:10; Joel 2:10, 31 and 3:15; and Amos 8:9), allow for a greater latitude of interpretations. They argue that Luke here is reminiscent of the Old Testament imagery, another way of saying the prophecies were fulfilled in Jesus.

The rending of the Temple veil also carries much symbolism. The high priest alone could enter the Holy of Holies. And even he entered by going past the veil only once a year when he offered a special sacrifice for the people's sins. Jesus' death once and for all removed the curtain that kept God and humanity apart.

Living in the days when the Temple curtain was in place meant living with unatoned sin until once a year the high priest made atonement for it, passed the curtain and entered the Holy of Holies. Otherwise there was a barrier in place, keeping God's people at a distance.

According to Hebrews 12:18-24, we can now enter, not just the Temple (which was an improvement on the experience at Mt. Sinai outlined in Heb. 12:18-21) but into the "the heavenly Jerusalem, the city of the living God . . . to angels in joyful assembly . . . to God . . . to Jesus the Mediator of a new covenant . . . ." Through faith in Jesus, we can come into God's presence clothed in the goodness and perfection of Jesus Himself. Hallelujah!

What did Jesus say on the cross? We speak traditionally of "the seven last words." No one gospel preserves all seven. Luke omitted Mark's "My God, my God, why have you forsaken me?" (Mk. 15:34; see Ps. 22:1), but His "Father, into your hands I commit my spirit" (vs. 46; see Ps. 31:5) gives us a different, complementary picture of the event. Luke stresses that Jesus did the Father's will in dying. This is much the same as Paul's teaching that reconciliation is the work of the Father in, or through, the Son (II Cor. 5:19). The Father was the active agent and the Son was the obedient instrument.

For Discussion

1. How should the rending of the Temple curtain affect your regular times of worshiping the Lord?

2. What is the connection between Christ's crucifixion and moral living? (See Gal. 2:17-21).

3. What are some ways to witness to someone who believes she will go to Heaven by living a "good" life?

Window on the Word

"This prayer of Jesus ["Father, forgive them," Lk. 23:34]

makes Him different from the Maccabean and many other Jewish martyrs. For example, in II Maccabees 7, we see an obvious contrast. The second Maccabean boy-martyr says to his persecutor, 'You accursed wretch, you dismiss us from this present life, but the King of the universe will raise us up to an everlasting renewal of life.' . . . The last (seventh) son declares, 'But you, who have contrived all sort of evil against the Hebrews, will certainly not escape the hands of God . . . you unholy wretch, you most defiled of all men, do not be elated in vain and puffed up by uncertain hope. . . ."

(J. Massyngbaerd Ford, in *My Enemy is My Guest*)

13

Standing Among His Disciples

Truth to Apply: Because the resurrection really happened, I have a place to stand and a message to share.

Key Verse: Look at my hands and my feet. It is myself! Touch me and see; a ghost does not have flesh and bones, as you see I have (Lk. 24:39).

In the early thirties, a young British lawyer, convinced that the Resurrection was a mere issue of fable and fantasy and sensing that it was the foundation stone of the Christian faith, decided to do the world a favor by once-and-for-all exposing this fraud and superstition. As a lawyer, he felt he had the critical faculties to sift evidence rigidly and to admit nothing as evidence that did not meet the stiff criteria for admission into a law court today.

While doing his research, a remarkable thing happened. The case was not nearly as easy as he had supposed. As a result, the first chapter of his book is entitled, "The Book That Refused to Be Written." In it he describes how, as he examined the evidence, he became persuaded, against his will, of the fact of the bodily resurrection of Christ.

The book is called, *Who Moved the Stone?* The author is Frank Morrison. (From *Know Why You Believe*, by Paul Little, Scripture Press.)

Where and how has Jesus so touched you that you *know* He's risen, alive, and present?

Background/Overview: *Luke 24:1-11, 36-53*

Upon first reading Luke 24:36-53, it may appear to the reader that all the events of the passage took place on a single day. Luke writes with such narrative skill that it seems as if the events taking place from the day of Christ's resurrection to the day of Ascension happened during a few hours. However, his purpose here is only to summarize several meetings with the disciples (not calling attention to when, where, etc.). In Acts 1:3, where his purposes were different, Luke affirms that the risen Christ appeared to His apostles during 40 days, meeting several times.

The passage for study in this chapter is a summary of all that Christ taught during His postresurrection days. Luke, thorough historian that he was, selected the teaching of Christ that underscored the purpose of his own writing: to give an account of all Jesus began to do and teach (Acts 1:1). Even so, commentators have tried to pinpoint exactly when Christ uttered His teaching in Luke 24:36-53. Some believe that the events of verses 36-43 took place on the night of His resurrection and that verses 44-48 represent His teaching over the 40 days He spent with them. The final verses, 49-53, are generally attributed to the day of His Ascension.

There is no need, however, for uncertainty about the time of this passage to be a stumbling block to Bible study. Apparently Luke did not think the precise timing of these events was important for the point he wanted to make.

In this passage, Luke gives a short, powerful reminder of the reality of Christ's resurrection and offers us a chance to study the resurrections centrality to the gospel message.

Light on the Text

In Their Midst (24:36-43)

Christ's appearance to His disciples was a frightening one. To understand the extent of their fears, we must back up a bit. The passage begins with the disciples gathered in a room. Earlier that morning the tomb had been found empty. Christ had also appeared to two followers on the road to Emmaus (Lk. 24:13-32), to Mary (Jn. 20:15-17), and to Peter (Lk. 24:34; I Cor. 15:5). These developments caused the disciples great confusion and made it necessary for them to meet and talk over the rumors. Too many unusual things were happening.

At the same time, the disciples feared for their lives; John says they hid behind a locked door (Jn. 20:19). He also says they were afraid of the Jews. Possibly, they believed that the authorities would not stop with Jesus and would hunt them down next.

Confused, fearful, they were rudderless. A good example of their attitude is expressed is Luke 24:21 by Cleopas when he said, ". . . but we had hoped that he was the one who was going to redeem Israel." It is no wonder that they were terrified by Christ's appearance in the room. They were tired, on edge, and the last thing they expected was to meet Christ.

John 20:19 states that Christ appeared in the room, apparently without unlocking the doors. Colin Chapman in *Christianity on Trial* puts it this way: "According to the accounts . . . there was some real continuity between His physical body during His lifetime and His body after the resurrection. But His resurrection body did not have all the limitations of a human body; it was not merely a resuscitated corpse."

One of Luke's specialties is highlighting the tenderness and compassion of Christ. These characteristics come out very clearly in this passage. Gently, Christ reproved those gathered in the locked room and questioned their doubt. Then the Savior and Shepherd began to show them the evidence of His physical reality.

The disciples did not understand; they thought Christ was a ghost. Could they have thought He was an evil spirit impersonating Christ? Another possibility is that they thought it was Christ's spirit coming back from the other world. Whatever they thought, in the words of the commentator Lenski, "Jesus makes the disciples learn what a resurrection body is like."

Christ offered what we might call material proof, calling on His followers to cast aside their doubts by seeing Him and touching Him. He invited them to view His scarred body, to touch it and to know that truly it was He, thereby refuting the belief that He was a ghost.

But even after touching Christ they could not believe. They were incredulous "because of joy and amazement." In other words, His appearance was so unexpected, so surprising to them (even though He had predicted it) that even after touching His wounds and hearing His voice, it was "too good to be true."

Christ then took something to eat. This would not only prove He was no ghost, but also remind them of the many times they had enjoyed the fellowship of eating together.

The Central Theme (24:44-48)

At the beginning of *Halley's Bible Handbook* it is stated in large letters that CHRIST IS THE CENTER AND HEART OF THE BIBLE. The early disciples now needed to see this even clearer than they had so far. Therefore, after giving the disciples experiential proof of His resurrection, Christ opened their minds so that they could understand the Old Testament Scriptures (vss. 45-47).

Jesus said that the Law of Moses, the Prophets, and the Psalms all foretold events that He fulfilled. These three names were like volume titles or section headings for the Old Testament. In effect He said that the whole Old Testament, in all its parts, foretold the events of the Gospel.

He gave the disciples insight into all the prophecies that He had fulfilled. But He did not merely tell of the prophecies; He explained them and, even more important, told how they related to repentance and forgiveness of sins.

Christ's death was an atonement for our sins and was prophesied in the Old Testament (Isa. 53). Our sin had separated us from God (Rom. 3:23) and the penalty for our sin is death (Rom. 6:23). Christ became a human and died in our place (Phil. 2:6-8; Rom. 5:8). He paid the penalty for us and was "raised to life for our justification" (Rom. 4:25). In order for us to receive God's forgiveness, we must repent (Mt. 3:2, 8; 4:17). Repentance and forgiveness have meaning only through Christ's work on the cross and through His resurrection.

The result of this new understanding was a commission. Christ sent the disciples out as witnesses, to preach in His name among all nations. Because they were witnesses of the fulfillment of divine prophecy, they were logical choices to begin what seemed to be an insurmountable task: to preach to the world. Their preaching would begin at

Jerusalem, the target city of Jesus' own strategy (see Lk. 9:51 and the whole movement of the Book from the early visits of Jesus to His entry into Jerusalem, trial, death, and resurrection). Jerusalem, therefore, was the launch city for world evangelism (Acts 1:8, which gives a geographical outline of Acts).

Parting From Them (24:49-53)

The task before the disciples was Herculean. But Christ offered them a new and extraordinary grace to help.

There are those who cast God in the role of a Creator who backs away from His Creation and allows it to run on its own. "We are to do the best we can" is the motto of those who think this way. But God did not leave us on our own to battle with sin and He did not merely offer help. His promise to the disciples was that they would be "clothed with power from on high." While Christ was preparing to *ascend*, the Holy Spirit was preparing to *descend*.

The command to stay in the city of Jerusalem was not just a test of obedience but was connected with the coming of the Holy Spirit. Only 10 days after the Ascension, the Holy Spirit would descend with power on the believers gathered in Jerusalem.

". . . What my Father has promised" was the Holy Spirit, the third person in the Godhead. The Holy Spirit was active in the Old Testament and in the gospels, but what Christ promised His disciples was the Spirit working in new ways. He came to dwell in the disciples as Comforter, Counselor, and Advocate. When the Holy Spirit was poured out at Pentecost, Peter cited the promise of Joel: "In the last days, God says, I will pour out my Spirit on all people" (Acts 2:17; Joel 2:28).

The departure of Christ was another growth point for the disciples. Instead of sadness, there was the opposite reaction: joy. For 40 days, Jesus prepared the disciples for His leaving. When the time came, it came without fanfare. He led them out as far as Bethany. After a blessing, He ascended into heaven.

When He ascended, He did so visibly. There was no vanishing (the opposite of His suddenly appearing in the room). His Ascension was public and observable. This may have been done in part to convince the disciples of the reality of the event. It was also to establish the basis for a strong hope for His equally visible return.

The joy the disciples felt upon their return to Jerusalem marked a strong contrast to their feelings of defeat, fear, and hopelessness 40 days earlier. The Resurrection and Ascension of Christ marked a turning point in their lives. From that time onward they were no longer bumbling men without direction. They became men of God and, as Christ had predicted, they were "clothed with power."

For Discussion

1. How is it possible for Christ to "open our minds" to Scripture today?

2. How would you compare your experience as a Christian to the experience of the early disciples?

3. What is the most helpful aspect of the Resurrection for you?

Window on the Word

Christ and Funerals

As a young man, D. L. Moody was called upon suddenly to preach a funeral sermon. He hunted all through the Four Gospels trying to find one of Christ's funeral sermons, but searched in vain. He found that Christ broke up every funeral He ever attended. Death could not exist where He was. When the dead heard His voice they sprang to life. Jesus said, "I am the resurrection, and the life."

Leader Helps and Lesson Plan

General Guidelines for Group Study

*Open and close each session with prayer.

*Since the lesson texts are not printed in the book, group members should have their Bibles with them for each study session.

*As the leader, prepare yourself for each session through personal study (during the week) of the Bible text and lesson. On notepaper, jot down any points of interest or concern as you study. Jot down your thoughts about how God is speaking to you through the text, and how He might want to speak to the entire group. Look up cross-reference passages (as they are referred to in the lessons), and try to find answers to questions that come to your mind. Also, recall stories from your own life experience that could be shared with the group to illustrate points in the lesson.

*Try to get participation from everyone. Get to know the more quiet members through informal conversation before and after the sessions. Then, during the study, watch for nonverbal signs (a change in expression or posture) that they would like to respond. Call on them. Say: "What are your thoughts on this, Sue?"

*Don't be afraid of silence. Adults need their own space. Often a long period of silence after a question means the group has been challenged to do some real thinking—hard work that can't be rushed!

*Acknowledge each contribution. No question is a dumb question. Every comment, no matter how "wrong," comes from a worthy person, who needs to be affirmed as valuable to the group. Find ways of tactfully accepting the speaker while guiding the discussion back on track: "Thank you for that comment, John; now what do some of the others think?" or, "I see your point, but are you aware of . . . ?"

When redirecting the discussion, however, be sensitive to the fact that sometimes the topic of the moment *should be* the "sidetrack" because it hits a felt need of the participants.

*Encourage *well-rounded* Christian growth. Christians are called to grow in knowledge of the Word, but they are also challenged to grow in love and wisdom. This means that they must constantly develop in their ability to wisely apply the Bible knowledge to their experience.

Lesson Plan

The following four-step lesson plan can be used effectively for each chapter, varying the different suggested approaches from lesson to lesson.

STEP 1: *Focus on Life Need*

The opening section of each lesson is an anecdote, quote, or other device designed to stimulate sharing on how the topic relates to practical daily living. There are many ways to do this. For example, you might list on the chalkboard the group's answers to: "How have you found this theme relevant to your daily life?" "What are your past successes, or failures, in this area?" "What is your present level of struggle or victory with this?" "Share a story from your own experience relating to this topic."

Sharing questions are designed to be open-ended and allow people to talk about themselves. The questions allow for sharing about past experiences, feelings, hopes and dreams, fears and anxieties, faith, daily life, likes and dislikes, sorrows and joys. Self-disclosure results in group members' coming to know each other at a more intimate level. This kind of personal sharing is necessary to experience deep affirmation and love.

However you do it, the point is to get group members to share *where they are now* in relation to the Biblical topic. As you seek to get the group involved, remember the following characteristics of good sharing questions:[1]

1. Good sharing questions encourage risk without forcing participants to go beyond their willingness to respond.

2. Good sharing questions begin with low risk and build toward higher risk. (It is often good, for instance, to ask a

history question to start, then build to present situations in people's lives.)

3. Sharing questions should not require people to confess their sins or to share only negative things about themselves.

4. Questions should be able to be answered by every member of the group.

5. The questions should help the group members to know one another better and learn to love and understand each other more.

6. The questions should allow for enough diversity in response so each member does not wind up saying the same thing.

7. They should ask for sharing of self, not for sharing of opinions.

STEP 2: *Focus on Bible Learning*

Use the *"Light on the Text"* section for this part of the lesson plan. Again, there are a number of ways to get group members involved, but the emphasis here is more on learning Bible content than on applying it. Below are some suggestions on how to proceed. The methods could be varied from week to week.

*Lecture on important points in the Bible passage (from your personal study notes).

*Assign specific verses in the Bible passage to individuals. Allow five or ten minutes for them to jot down 1) questions, 2) comments, 3) points of concern raised by the text. Then have them share in turn what they have written down.

*Pick important or controversial verses from the passage. In advance, do a personal study to find differences of interpretation among commentators. List and explain these "options" on a blackboard and invite comments concerning the relative merits of each view. Summarize and explain your own view, and challenge other group members to further study.

*Have class members do their own outline of the Bible passage. This is done by giving an original title to each section, chapter, and paragraph, placing each under its appropriate heading according to subject matter. Share the outlines and discuss.

*Make up your own sermons from the Bible passage. Each sermon could include: Title, Theme Sentence, Outline, Illustration, Application, Benediction. Share and discuss.

*View works of art based on the text. Discuss.

*Individually, or as a group, paraphrase the Bible passage in your own words. Share and discuss.

*Have a period of silent meditation upon the Bible passage. Later, share insights.

STEP 3: *Focus on Bible Application*

Most adults prefer group discussion above any other learning method. Use the "For Discussion" section for each lesson to guide a good discussion on the lesson topic and how it relates to felt needs.

Students can benefit from discussion in a number of important ways:

1. Discussion stimulates interest and thinking, and helps students develop the skills of observation, analysis, and hope.

2. Discussion helps students clarify and review what they have learned.

3. Discussion allows students to hear opinions that are more mature and perhaps more Christlike than their own.

4. Discussion stimulates creativity and aids students in applying what they have learned.

5. When students verbalize what they believe and are forced to explain or defend what they say, their convictions are strengthened and their ability to share what they believe with others is increased.

There are many different ways to structure a discussion. All have group interaction as their goal. All provide an opportunity to share in the learning process.

But using different structures can add surprise to a discussion. It can mix people in unique ways. It can allow new people to talk.

Total Class Discussion

In some small classes, all students are able to participate in one effective discussion. This can build a sense of class unity, and it allows everyone to hear the wisdom of peers. But in most groups, total class discussion by itself is unsatisfactory because there is usually time for only a few to contribute.

Buzz Groups

Small groups of three to ten people are assigned any topic for discussion. They quickly select a chairperson and a secretary. The chairperson is responsible for keeping the discussion on track, and the secretary records the group's ideas, reporting the relevant ones to the total class.

Brainstorming

Students, usually in small groups, are presented with a problem and asked to come up with as many different solutions as possible. Participants should withhold judgment until all suggestions (no matter how creative!) have been offered. After a short break, the group should pick the best contribution from those suggested and refine it. Each brainstorming group will present its solution in a total class discussion.

Forum Discussion

Forum discussion is especially valuable when the subject is difficult and the students would not be able to participate in a meaningful discussion without quite a bit of background. People with special training or experience have insights which would not ordinarily be available to the students. Each forum member should prepare a three- to five-minute speech and be given uninterrupted time in which to present it. Then students should be encouraged to interact with the speakers, either directly or through a forum moderator.

Debate

As students prepare before class for their parts in a debate, they should remember that it is the affirmative side's responsibility to prove that the resolve is correct. The negative has to prove that it isn't. Of course, the negative may also want to present an alternative proposal.

There are many ways to structure a debate, but the following pattern is quite effective.

1. First affirmative speech
2. First negative speech
3. Second affirmative speech
4. Second negative speech
   (brief break while each side plans its rebuttal)
5. First negative rebuttal
6. First affirmative rebuttal
7. Second negative rebuttal
8. Second affirmative rebuttal.

Floating Panel

Sometimes you have a topic to which almost everyone in the room would have something to contribute, for example: marriage, love, work, getting along with people. For a change of pace, have a floating panel: four or five people, whose names are chosen at random, will become "experts" for several minutes. These people sit in chairs in the front of the room while you and other class members ask them questions. The questions should be experience related. When the panel has been in front for several minutes, enough time for each person to make several comments, draw other names and replace the original members.

Interview As Homework

Ask students to interview someone during the week and present what they learned in the form of short reports the following Sunday.

Interview in Class

Occasionally it is profitable to schedule an in-class interview, perhaps with a visiting missionary or with someone who has unique insights to share with the group. One person can take charge of the entire interview, structuring and asking questions. But whenever possible the entire class should take part. Each student should write a question to ask the guest.

In-Group Interview

Divide the class into groups of three, called triads. Supply all groups with the same question or discussion topic. A in the group interviews B while C listens. Then B interviews C while A listens. Finally C interviews A while B listens. Each interview should take from one to three minutes. When the triads return to the class, each person reports on what was heard rather than said.

Following every class period in which you use discussion, ask yourself these questions to help determine the success of your discussion time:

1. In what ways did this discussion contribute to the group's understanding of today's lesson?

2. If each person was not involved, what can I do next week to correct the situation?

3. In what ways did content play a role in the discussion? (I.e., people were not simply sharing off-the-top-of-their-head opinions.)

4. What follow-up, if any, should be made on the discussion? (For example, if participants showed a lack of knowledge, or misunderstanding in some area of Scripture, you may want to cover this subject soon during the class hour. Or, if they discussed decisions they were making or projects they felt the class should be involved in, follow-up outside the class hour may be necessary.)

STEP 4: *Focus on Life Response*

This step tries to incorporate a bridge from the Bible lesson to actual daily living. It should be a *specific* suggestion as to "how we are going to *do* something about this," either individually, or as a group. Though this is a goal to aim for, it is unlikely that everyone will respond to every lesson. But it is good to have a suggested life response ready for that one or two in the group who may have been moved by *this* lesson to respond *this week* in a tangible way.

Sometimes a whole group will be moved by one particular lesson to do a major project in light of their deepened understanding of, and commitment to, God's will. Such a response would be well worth the weeks of study that may have preceded it.

Examples of life response activities:

1. A whole class, after studying Scriptural principles of evangelism, decides to host an outreach Bible study in a new neighborhood.

2. As a result of studying one of Paul's prayers for the Ephesians, a group member volunteers to start and oversee a church prayer chain for responding to those in need.

3. A group member invites others to join her in memorizing the key verse for the week.

4. Two group members, after studying portions of the Sermon on the Mount, write and perform a song about peacemaking.

Obviously, only you and your group can decide how to respond appropriately to the challenge of living for Christ daily. But the possibilities are endless.

[1]From *Using the Bible in Groups,* by Roberta Hestenes.
© Roberta Hestenes 1983. Adapted and used by permission of Westminster Press, Philadelphia, PA.
[2]The material on discussion methods is adapted from *Creative Teaching Methods,* by Marlene D. LeFever, available from your local Christian bookstore or from David C. Cook Publishing Co., 850 N. Grove Ave., Elgin, IL 60120. Order number: 25254. $14.95. This book contains step-by-step directions for dozens of methods appropriate for use in adult classes.